UNDERSTANDING THE MASS

UNDERSTANDING
THE MASS

100 QUESTIONS | 100 ANSWERS

MIKE AQUILINA

Copyright ©2011 Mike Aquilina.
PUBLISHED BY SERVANT
An Imprint of Viident

All rights reserved.

Scripture passages have been taken from the *Revised Standard Version*, Catholic edition. Copyright 1946, 1952, 1971 by the Division of Christian Education of the National Council of Churches of Christ in the USA. Used by permission. All rights reserved. Quotes are taken from the English translation of the *Catechism of the Catholic Church* for the United States of America (indicated as *CCC*), 2nd ed. Copyright 1997 by United States Catholic Conference—Libreria Editrice Vaticana. Quotations from the early Church Fathers are taken from the great collections produced in the nineteenth century: the *Ante-Nicene Fathers* and the *Nicene and Post-Nicene Fathers*. These series emerged originally from the University of Edinburgh in Scotland, and so they are often referred to as the "Edinburgh Edition" of the Fathers. The English language has undergone major changes since these were published, so the author has taken the liberty of updating the translations, after consulting other translations and, whenever possible, the texts in the original languages.

Cover by Candle Light Studios
Cover image © istockphoto.com | Kryczka
Book design by Mark Sullivan

Previous edition ISBN: 978-0-86716-949-2 (softcover)

LIBRARY OF CONGRESS CATALOGING-IN-PUBLICATION DATA
Aquilina, Mike.
Understanding the Mass : 100 questions, 100 answers / Mike Aquilina.
p. cm.
Includes bibliographical references (p.   ) and index.
ISBN 978-0-86716-949-2 (alk. paper)
1. Mass—Miscellanea. 2. Lord's Supper—Catholic Church—Miscellanea.
I. Title.
BX2230.3.A68 2011
234'.163—dc22

2011013237

ISBN: 978-1-63582-352-3 (softcover)
ISBN: 978-1-63582-306-6 (eBook)

Printed in the United States of America

CONTENTS

INTRODUCTION | *xi*

THE FIRST MASS | *1*

BASICS OF THE MASS | *3*
1. Why do we call our worship "the Mass"?
2. What other names does the Mass go by?
3. What happens at a Catholic Mass?
4. Why do we need this ritual? Can't I worship God just as well using my own words?
5. Why does the Mass refer to Jesus as a "victim" and a "lamb"?
6. Why is the Mass a sacrifice?
7. Why is the Mass the same sacrifice that Christ made on the cross?
8. Is every Catholic worship service a Mass?

THE EUCHARIST: THE REAL PRESENCE OF CHRIST | *11*

9. What is the Eucharist?
10. What is the real presence?
11. If God is everywhere, what's special about the real presence in the Eucharist?
12. Why do Catholics believe in the real presence, instead of just saying that the bread and wine are symbols?
13. What is transubstantiation?
14. When does transubstantiation happen?
15. Why does the priest mix water with the wine?
16. If the Body of Christ is in every Catholic church, does that mean Jesus has lots of bodies all over the world?
17. How can we teach children about the real presence?

SCRIPTURAL AND HISTORIC ROOTS | *21*

18. Where does the Mass appear in the Bible?
19. How can the Mass appear in the Old Testament if Jesus instituted it in the New?
20. What are the Jewish roots of the Christian ritual?
21. Where does the Mass appear in the New Testament?
22. How did Jesus prepare his followers for the institution of the Mass?
23. Why do the accounts of the first Mass differ from book to book?
24. How do we know that Jesus intended the Church to continue offering the Mass?
25. Did the early Church—the persecuted, "underground" Church—celebrate the Mass? If so, how?

THE CELEBRANT | 45

26. Who may offer the Mass?
27. How did Jesus give our priests the power to change bread and wine into his body and blood?
28. What is a pontifical Mass?
29. Is Mass with the pope or bishop "worth more" than Mass in my parish?
30. Does there have to be a congregation for there to be a Mass?
31. What are the vestments the priest wears?
32. Why does the priest wear vestments?
33. What do the colors of the vestments mean?

OBLIGATION AND OPPORTUNITY | 51

34. How often must I go to Mass?
35. Why does the Church require us to go to Mass on Sunday?
36. Can I satisfy the Sunday obligation by going to Vespers instead of Mass?
37. What does it mean to offer the Mass for a particular "intention"?
38. Why do Catholics offer Masses for the dead?
39. How does the Mass relate to the other sacraments?
40. What is the relationship between the Mass and social justice?
41. How is the Mass like heaven?

Rites | 63

42. Why do some Catholic churches celebrate the Eucharist in ways that are far different from the way I know?
43. What is the Latin Mass?
44. What is the Tridentine Mass or Extraordinary Form?
45. Why do some Catholics like the Latin Mass so much?
46. Why is Latin still the official language of the Mass in the Catholic Church?
47. Do non-Catholic churches also celebrate the Mass?

Properly Equipped | 69

48. Why does the Church use unleavened bread?
49. May the priest use other types of bread?
50. May a priest use gluten-free wheat bread for the sake of people who have celiac disease?
51. What if my body can't take any wheat at all?
52. What are the vessels used in the Mass?
53. What's special about altar candles?
54. What are rubrics?
55. What's hidden in the compartment in or under many altars?
56. Why does the Church honor the relics of the saints?

Receiving Communion | 77

57. Who may receive Holy Communion?
58. How should I prepare to go to Mass and receive Communion?
59. What is the Communion fast?
60. What if I forget and break the Communion fast?
61. What happens if I receive Communion in a state of mortal sin?

62. How should I receive Communion?
63. Why do some people receive Communion on the hand and others on the tongue?
64. Is it better to receive Communion under both species? Do I receive "more" if I do?
65. What is *viaticum*?
66. Can the Church deny Communion to particular individuals? If so, when and how?
67. Why are certain politicians allowed to take Communion even when they vote against Church teachings?
68. What is excommunication?
69. How often may I go to Communion?
70. How often must I go to Communion?
71. What should I do after taking Communion?
72. What should I do if I attend Mass but cannot go, or choose not to go, to Communion?
73. Are Catholics allowed to take Communion in a non-Catholic church?
74. Are non-Catholics allowed to take Communion in a Catholic church?

THE PARTS OF THE MASS | *91*

75. How is the Mass divided?
76. Why does the Mass begin with the Sign of the Cross?
77. What is the Penitential Rite?
78. Why do we pray to Mary and the saints?
79. What is the Gloria?
80. How does the Church pick the Bible readings for each Mass?
81. What is the Alleluia?

82. What is the gesture people make before the reading of the Gospel?
83. What is a sermon supposed to be?
84. What is the Creed?
85. What is the Universal Prayer?
86. Why does the Church collect money at Mass?
87. What is the Offertory?
88. What is the Eucharistic Prayer?
89. What is the Canon of the Mass?
90. What is the Preface?
91. What is the "Holy, Holy, Holy"?
92. What is the institution narrative?
93. Why does the Church call upon the Holy Spirit at this point in the Mass?
94. What is the "mystery of faith"?
95. What is the Communion Rite?
96. Why do we pray the Lord's Prayer at this part of the Mass?
97. What is the "Lord, I am not worthy" prayer?
98. What is Holy Communion?
99. Why does the Mass end so abruptly after Communion?
100. What should I do after Mass?

NOTES | *115*

Introduction

To Catholics nothing is as common as the Mass. It's ordinary, and it's routine. It's the one thing the Church requires us to attend regularly. It's familiar, a family event.

Yet it's also enigmatic—even to Catholics, when they stop to think about it. The priests wear unusual clothing that would draw strange looks if worn in public. The banquet is served from antiquated vessels made from precious metal. People make ritual gestures and strike postures that would be out of place at work or at home. They speak in a language that's highly symbolic, referring to an historical person as a "lamb."

Why do Catholics do what they do? What do these practices mean?

The questions occur even to Catholics these days as a new edition of the missal, the book of Mass prayers, is introduced to the English-speaking world. We recite the ancient prayers in slightly different form, and they appear suddenly new to us. The texts used in this book are those approved by the Vatican for the missal whose use is standard as of Advent 2011.

The Mass may be routine, and it may be the common property of millions of Catholics, from all nations, from all social classes, for two thousand years. But it's not a simple reality. It's profound. It's rich. It's thick with symbolism. Its theology reaches out to touch the small details of ordinary life, including home and work and leisure. Its vision, meanwhile, stretches as high as heaven, and its power touches the depths of purgatory. Its typical worshippers include a cross section of society, from the wealthiest to the homeless, as well as countless hosts of angels and saints. Its words and postures and gestures have deep historical roots and profound mystical meanings.

This book answers the most common questions about the Mass—and anticipates dozens of others that are less often heard but fascinating nonetheless. It ranges from the sublime to the silly—at least in the minds of people who are afraid to ask.

This book deals with practical and doctrinal questions about the Mass, moving from the basics to the more theological. It describes the various participants in the drama (the clergy, the laity, and God) and the proper "equipment," so to speak, including vessels and vestments. The final chapter walks through the Mass, step by step, describing the drama of the ritual, the words and the movements.

So follow your curiosity and your sense of wonder. If you're a Catholic, you may be surprised by how much you've missed in the Mass or taken for granted. If you're not Catholic, you'll get a glimpse of the glory that holds Catholics in thrall, so that even if you can't embrace it yourself, you can at least understand why Catholics can't let it go.

The First Mass

Now as they were eating, Jesus took bread, and blessed, and broke it, and gave it to the disciples and said, "Take, eat; this is my body." And he took a chalice, and when he had given thanks he gave it to them, saying, "Drink of it, all of you; for this is my blood of the covenant, which is poured out for many for the forgiveness of sins. I tell you I shall not drink again of this fruit of the vine until that day when I drink it new with you in my Father's kingdom."

And when they had sung a hymn, they went out to the Mount of Olives. (Matthew 26:26–30)

BASICS OF THE MASS

1. Why do we call our worship "the Mass"?

The word *Mass* is really an accident of history.

In the early days of Christianity, only the baptized were allowed to witness the Eucharist. After the Liturgy of the Word—the first part of our Mass, in which we hear the Scripture readings and the homily—the unbaptized were sent home with the words *"Ite, missa est"*—roughly, "Go; you are dismissed." Christians knew that important division in the service as the *missa*, the dismissal. Soon they began to use the word *missa* for the whole service of the Eucharist that followed the dismissal and then for the entire worship. Our English word *Mass* comes from that Latin word *missa*.

The words *Ite, missa est* are still used to conclude the Mass when it is celebrated in Latin.

2. What other names does the Mass go by?

We often call it the liturgy, from a Greek word meaning "public service," although technically the word *liturgy* also includes all the prescribed rites of the Church, including the ones that take place outside the Mass. In Eastern traditions the Mass is often called the Divine Liturgy.

We also sometimes say "the Eucharist," which refers more specifically to the part of the Mass where the sacrament of the Eucharist is celebrated.

We call the Mass the Holy Sacrifice because the Eucharist makes the sacrifice of Christ on the cross present to us on our altar (see question 6, Why is the Mass a sacrifice?). We call it the Lord's Supper because it looks back to the Last Supper and forward to the marriage supper of the Lamb (see Revelation 19).

There are many particular styles of Masses that come from different Christian cultures and different times, and they have particular names.

The *Novus Ordo* ("New Order") is a name sometimes used for the form of the Mass that was adopted by the Western Catholic Church after the Second Vatican Council; because some schismatic traditionalists have used *Novus Ordo* pejoratively, many Catholics dislike the term, preferring to call it the "ordinary form."

The *Tridentine Mass* was the common form of Mass used in the West from the Council of Trent in the middle 1500s until the Second Vatican Council; it can still be used by any Roman Catholic priest. (See question 44, What is the Tridentine Mass or Extraordinary Form?)

The Eastern Churches celebrate Mass according to different ritual forms, depending on the traditions of their culture of origin—Byzantine, Ukrainian, Chaldean, Coptic, and so on.

But although there are multiple styles of the Mass and multiple names for it, there is only one Mass. It may change clothes as it moves from country to country or age to age, but the Mass is always fundamentally the same, with the same elements and the same miracle of meeting Christ face to face at its heart.

3. What happens at a Catholic Mass?

At every Catholic Mass the sacrifice of Jesus on the cross is made present on the altar; it is re-presented, not as a symbol but in reality and in the fullness of truth. That's the short answer.

The longer answer is that there's a certain ritual we go through at every Mass. Though some of the details change, the main parts of the ritual are always the same and have been century after century, going all the way back to the time of the apostles.

This prescribed ritual is what we call the *liturgy*. Each part of the liturgy has a meaning, and the more you know about those meanings, the more you'll understand and be fascinated by the Mass that goes on in your own parish church.

4. Why do we need this ritual? Can't I worship God just as well using my own words?

Praying to God in our own words is good, and we can hardly do it often enough. But it's not all we need.

We could answer the question by saying that Jesus told us to use a ritual, and that's that. At the Last Supper he gave the apostles explicit instructions to repeat the breaking of the bread and the passing of the cup (see Luke 22:19). But that wouldn't really be an answer. Jesus did nothing without a reason.

Rituals are what keep us on the right track. They can include the habits we learned as children, like the way we get dressed in the morning or the way we eat a pizza. We have a set way of answering a phone call, of ending a letter, of greeting the queen of England. The most important things we do—eating, being born, being married, dying—are surrounded by ritual.

We have all these rituals because it's not possible for us to think through everything we do. We don't decide when to breathe or when to beat our hearts in order to pump the proper amount of blood. Our bodies are wisely designed to take care of these processes automatically. Rituals likewise help us toward an appropriate reverence and love for God.

We also have rituals to convey certain messages to other people. What we do is really as much a part of communication as our spoken language. Someone we meet may say, "Pleased to meet you," while shaking our hand; the person sends a different message if he says exactly the same thing while thumbing his nose. Shaking hands is a ritual that conveys a certain meaning; for that matter, so is thumbing your nose. Rituals are part of the way we communicate, and they often speak louder than our words.

Each part of our liturgy—the collection of rituals that make up our worship—has a particular meaning. These meanings have been refined over many centuries, but—just like many of our social rituals—the core goes back to the beginning.

5. Why does the Mass refer to Jesus as a "victim" and a "lamb"?

We call Jesus a victim because he offered himself as a sacrifice for our sins.

A sacrifice is an offering made to God by a priest. In Old Testament times the Israelites offered many different kinds of sacrifices to God for many different purposes. But the main point of a sacrifice is always the same: It acknowledges that God rules all creation and that everything we have really belongs to him.

The death of Jesus Christ on the cross is the perfect and final sacrifice. Of course, the people who killed him weren't intending to offer a sacrifice. They were intending to kill a wandering preacher who had started to annoy them. But Jesus, our High Priest, offered himself to be killed as a sacrifice. "On the part of those who killed him," St. Thomas Aquinas explains, "the suffering of Christ was an evil; but on the part of the one who suffered out of love, it was a sacrifice."[1]

In Old Testament times a lamb was the sacrifice offered at Passover, the feast of unleavened bread (see Exodus 12 and question 48, Why does the Church use unleavened bread?). When Jesus came to the Jordan to be baptized, John the Baptist recognized who he was instantly: "Behold, the Lamb of God, who takes away the sin of the world!" (John 1:29).

Christ is our Passover lamb, as St. Paul explicitly told the Corinthians: "Christ, our Paschal Lamb, has been sacrificed. Let us, therefore, celebrate the festival, not with the old leaven, the leaven of malice and evil, but with the unleavened bread of sincerity and truth" (1 Corinthians 5:7–8).

St. Peter makes the same connection for us: "You know that you were ransomed from the futile ways inherited from your fathers, not with perishable things such as silver or gold, but with the precious blood of Christ, like that of a lamb without blemish or spot" (1 Peter 1:18–19).

In John's vision recorded in the book of Revelation, Christ appears again as a lamb: "And between the throne and the four living creatures and among the elders, I saw a Lamb standing, as though it had been slain" (Revelation 5:6). Although the Lamb here has been "slain," he is very much alive. And John sees preparations for a wedding feast:

> Then I heard what seemed to be the voice of a great multitude, like the sound of many waters and like the sound of mighty thunderpeals, crying,
>   "Hallelujah! For the Lord our God the Almighty reigns.
>   Let us rejoice and exult and give him the glory,
>   for the marriage of the Lamb has come,
>   and his Bride has made herself ready;
>   it was granted her to be clothed with fine linen, bright and pure"—
> for the fine linen is the righteous deeds of the saints.
>   And the angel said to me, "Write this: Blessed are those who are invited to the marriage supper of the Lamb." And he said to me, "These are true words of God." (Revelation 19:6–9)

The bride is the Church, and the marriage supper is the eternal worship of God in heaven. We participate in that celebration when we participate in the Mass.

6. Why is the Mass a sacrifice?

The Mass is a sacrifice because it makes present to us, right here in our own parish church, the sacrifice of Christ on the cross.

That doesn't mean the priest is somehow killing Jesus again or that there needs to be *another* sacrifice after Jesus died on the cross. There is *one* sacrifice of Jesus for all time and for all people. But we're dealing with eternity here. That *one* sacrifice is present to us on our altar at every Mass. We see the Body and Blood of Christ offered today because Christ is living and eternal.

7. Why is the Mass the same sacrifice that Christ made on the cross?

It's the same sacrifice because both the offering and the one who offers it are the same. Christ, our "great high priest" (Hebrews 4:14), offered his own flesh and blood to be sacrificed on the cross. Acting through his priests, Christ today offers his own flesh and blood to be sacrificed on our altars. Because Christ is eternal God, his sacrifice is eternal. Even though the sacrifice of the Mass is "unbloody," as generations of catechumens have learned to say, it is the same as the bloody sacrifice Christ made of himself on the cross.

8. Is every Catholic worship service a Mass?

No. There are services of prayer in which there is no Eucharist. The evening service called Vespers, for example, consists of prayers, hymns, and Scripture readings but no breaking of bread. In small or remote Catholic communities where there is no resident priest, laypeople may gather for prayer services or Communion services, but these are not Masses. The service is a Mass if the entire liturgy of the Mass is celebrated, including the consecration of the bread and wine.

The Eucharist: The Real Presence of Christ

9. What is the Eucharist?

The Eucharist is the sacrament at the heart of the Mass, in which bread and wine become the Body and Blood of Christ. It was instituted by Christ at the Last Supper. Whenever the Eucharist is celebrated, the sacrifice of Christ on the cross is made present to us on the altar.

The word *Eucharist* comes from a Greek word meaning "thanksgiving." The Eucharist is, foremost, a sacrifice of thanksgiving to God for our salvation. In fact, the same Greek word was often used to translate the Hebrew term we translate as "sacrifice of thanksgiving" in the psalms (see Psalm 50:14, 23; 116:17).

We use the term *Holy Communion* because in the Eucharist all believers are brought together in communion with Christ to form one body.

10. What is the real presence?

The real presence is the presence of Christ in the consecrated bread and wine. Catholics know that Jesus Christ is present, whole and entire, under the forms of bread and wine. Body and blood, soul and divinity—the bread and wine *are* changed into Christ.

This is one of the important differences between Catholics and most Protestants. To most of our Protestant brothers and sisters, the Eucharist is a *symbolic* meal in which the bread and wine somehow remind them of the sacrifice of Christ. But for Catholics the bread and wine *are* Christ; they're not just symbols of Christ.

11. If God is everywhere, what's special about the real presence in the Eucharist?

When we say "real presence," we don't mean to imply that Christ—who is God—isn't really present throughout the universe. But the real presence in the Eucharist is fuller and more complete. Only in the Eucharist is Christ really present *in body and blood, soul and divinity,* and only there do we meet Christ completely.

12. Why do Catholics believe in the real presence, instead of just saying that the bread and wine are symbols?

We believe in the real presence because we accept the words of Christ in Scripture. Jesus was not ambiguous when he told his disciples what he was doing:

> Now as they were eating, Jesus took bread, and blessed, and broke it, and gave it to the disciples and said, "Take, eat; this is my body." And he took a chalice, and when he had given thanks he gave it to them, saying, "Drink of it, all of you; for this is my blood of the covenant, which is poured out for many for the forgive-

ness of sins. I tell you I shall not drink again of this fruit of the vine until that day when I drink it new with you in my Father's kingdom." (Matthew 26:26–29)

Long before the Last Supper, Jesus had told his disciples what to expect. In what we call the "Bread of Life discourse," Jesus shocked most of his followers by telling them they were going to have to eat his flesh and drink his blood.

> "This is the bread which comes down from heaven, that a man may eat of it and not die. I am the living bread which came down from heaven; if any one eats of this bread, he will live for ever; and the bread which I shall give for the life of the world is my flesh."
>
> The Jews then disputed among themselves, saying, "How can this man give us his flesh to eat?" So Jesus said to them, "Truly, truly, I say to you, unless you eat the flesh of the Son of man and drink his blood, you have no life in you; he who eats my flesh and drinks my blood has eternal life, and I will raise him up at the last day. For my flesh is food indeed, and my blood is drink indeed. He who eats my flesh and drinks my blood abides in me, and I in him. As the living Father sent me, and I live because of the Father, so he who eats me will live because of me. This is the bread which came down from heaven, not such as the fathers ate and died; he who eats this bread will live for ever." (John 6:50–58)

When Jesus has been so completely straightforward and explicit, it's hard to think that he was speaking metaphorically. The Catholic Church believes that Jesus Christ meant what he said, that the bread and wine really are his body and blood.

13. What is transubstantiation?

Transubstantiation is how Christ comes to be really present in the Eucharist. The doctrine of the *real presence,* as we saw in question 10, holds that the bread and wine really do become the Body and Blood of Christ at the moment of consecration; *transubstantiation* is a word that describes that change.

It's a big word, and it can seem a little frightening. It was coined in the Middle Ages to describe what the Church had always believed about the Eucharist. At that time the Church found it necessary to be very specific and technical because some people had begun to doubt that when Christ said, "This is my body," and, "This is my blood," he meant what he said.

Earlier Christian writers had addressed the subject, of course. St. Ignatius of Antioch, whose writings represent one of the oldest Christian testimonies outside the Bible, pointed out that the very mark of heresy was to deny that the Eucharist is the "flesh" of the Savior.[1] Even as early as AD 107, when Ignatius wrote his letters, true Christians held that Jesus meant what he said: The bread and wine were his body and blood.

In the fourth century, St. Gregory of Nyssa, St. Cyril of Jerusalem, and others were already struggling to come up with a word that would describe what happened when the bread and wine were consecrated. St. Gregory offered several terms, none of which quite caught on. The important thing, of course, is that he took the *fact* for granted: Christians had always known that the bread and wine really did change into the Body and Blood of Christ, and the only question was how to describe the change.

In the high Middle Ages, however, some philosophers began to question whether *really* meant, you know, "really." Were the bread and wine *really* the Body and Blood of Christ? Perhaps the Eucharist was only a symbolic ceremony, meant to *remind* us that Christ had died for us.

At about the same time, the philosophical works of Aristotle were causing quite a stir among the best thinkers of the age. Forgotten for centuries and only recently rediscovered, Aristotle suddenly seemed like the man with all the answers for problems in philosophy and science. His precise distinctions in terminology made it possible to talk about things that even the best thinkers struggled to find words to describe. So when the best thinkers in the Church set out to define exactly what happens in the Eucharist, they naturally borrowed Aristotle's language and his way of thinking. They started to talk about *substance* and *accidents*.

To speak like an Aristotelian, the *substance* of a thing is the reality, or thing itself, made up of matter and form. Every substance has *accidents*, which are properties that are not essential to the substance, such as color.

I can paint a board red. I can stick it in the freezer and make it cold. But it's still a piece of wood. A philosopher might say that I've changed the *accidents* of the board—its color and its temperature, in this case—without changing the *substance*.

With the bread and wine of the Eucharist, on the other hand, the accidents remain the same. The bread and wine still look, feel, and taste like bread and wine. But the *substance*—what the bread and wine really are—has changed completely, from bread and wine to body and blood. That's what the word *transubstantiation* means.

We say that the Body and Blood of Christ are *really present* "under the species of the bread and wine," *species* meaning "appearances." That change happens at the moment of consecration, when the priest repeats the words of Christ, "This is my body," and "This is my blood."

14. When does transubstantiation happen?

Transubstantiation happens at the consecration, when the priest speaks the words of Christ: "This is my body," and "This is my blood." These are the words Christ used to make the transformation at the Last Supper, and the priest at our Mass stands in the place of Christ, speaking the same words.

15. Why does the priest mix water with the wine?

There are two answers to this question.

The first answer is that that's how people served wine at the time of the Last Supper and for a long time afterward. Vintners made wine very strong, like juices that we buy today in concentrated form. Wine was diluted with water at a civilized table (see Proverbs 9:5); only barbarians drank unmixed wine.

The second answer is that this custom of humble and ordinary beginnings has acquired a rich symbolic meaning. Some of the earliest Christian writers—as early as St. Justin Martyr in AD 150—mention the "mixed cup." Some speak of it only in passing, but some also discuss its significance.

For some the wine and water represent the blood and water that poured from Jesus' side on the cross. After the soldiers broke the legs of the thieves who had been crucified with Jesus, they "saw that he was already dead," and "they did not break his legs. But one of the soldiers pierced his side with a spear, and at once there came out blood and water" (John 19:31–34). As the priest pours the two elements, a devout Christian can't help but remember this scene from the Scriptures.

Other interpreters saw the mixture as a symbol of God's communion with us. St. Clement of Alexandria, writing around AD 200, emphasized the effects of Communion upon the individual who receives: "As wine is blended with water, so is the Spirit with man."[2] A few years later, in North Africa, St. Cyprian spoke of the mixed cup but emphasized Christ's communion with the *whole Church*:

> The water is understood as the people, while the wine shows forth the blood of Christ. When the water is mingled in the cup with wine, the people are united with Christ.... Once the water and wine are mingled in the Lord's cup, the mixture cannot any more be separated. Even so, nothing can separate the Church...from Christ.[3]

There is something exact about the symbol: Christ is the wine; we are the bit of water. The main part of the sacrament is Christ really present, but communion does not happen without our willing participation.

The mixed chalice can also be seen as a sign of Christ's two natures, divine and human, united in one person. The wine represents his divinity, the water his humanity. The two natures come to us together in the Eucharist, as they did in the Incarnation.

Thus from earliest times the mixed chalice at Mass was emblematic of the mystery it held: the mystery of Christ and of salvation by his blood.

The Church has insisted on this mixing of the water with the wine for two millennia. In the sixteenth century the Council of Trent even excommunicated priests who neglected to mix the elements. The Church has good reasons to be faithful here. Some are perhaps historical: a fidelity to a custom dating back to the time of Jesus. Others, however, are doctrinal, dealing with the mystery at the heart of the faith: the marvelous exchange spelled out in the prayer at the Offertory: "By the mystery of this water and wine, may we come to share in the divinity of Christ, who humbled himself to share in our humanity."

16. If the Body of Christ is in every Catholic church, does that mean Jesus has lots of bodies all over the world?

No. There is only one body of Christ. Jesus Christ is God, and his resurrected body has been glorified. That means it's no longer subject to the limitations of our earthly bodies. As God, Christ is present everywhere but is still only one.

17. How can we teach children about the real presence?

First of all, we can simply tell them that Jesus is really present in the sacrament. Children are capable of understanding that at a very young age. They may ask difficult questions,

The Eucharist: The Real Presence of Christ

but they'll have no trouble understanding the idea.

To answer some of those difficult questions, we can teach by analogy. For example, when you eat an orange, your body changes that orange into flesh and blood. Does your skin or your blood look anything like that orange? No, but the orange has gone through a wonderful—almost miraculous—change, and the nutrition in it has become part of you. If it was possible for that orange to become something completely different, purely by natural processes acting in our bodies, then it's not hard for God to change bread and wine miraculously into the Body and Blood of Christ.

Not all learning is intellectual though. In fact, children usually learn far more from what they observe than from what we try to tell them. As with most other principles of religion, one of the best ways to teach our children about the real presence is by our own example. If our children see us living what we believe, they know that we really mean it, and they know what those beliefs mean in action in our lives.

For example, we can take our children with us to Eucharistic adoration and let them participate with us. If they see us behaving with all the reverence we ought to show in the presence of Christ on the altar, they'll know that we really believe what we tell them about the Eucharist. They'll know what the "real presence" means: that Christ is really there in front of us.

Scriptural and Historic Roots

18. Where does the Mass appear in the Bible?
The Mass actually appears throughout the Bible, in the Old Testament as well as in the New. We celebrate the Mass precisely because we're continuing the worship of God that went on in Scriptural times.

And if you read Scripture at all, you'll see that it's equally true that the Bible appears throughout the Mass. A large proportion of the words of our liturgy come directly from Scripture. There is continuity between biblical worship and our own.

19. How can the Mass appear in the Old Testament if Jesus instituted it in the New?
God is the Author of all history. Although Christ gave us the specific instructions for the Mass at the Last Supper, all of history had been preparing humanity for that moment. We see foreshadowings—what Bible scholars call "types"—of the Mass throughout the Old Testament.

For example, when Abraham returned from rescuing Lot and the four kings, Melchizedek, the priest-king of Salem (later called Jerusalem), brought him an offering of bread and wine.

> And Melchizedek king of Salem brought out bread and wine; he was priest of God Most High. And he blessed him and said,
> "Blessed be Abram by God Most High,
> maker of heaven and earth;
> and blessed be God Most High,
> who has delivered your enemies into your hand!"
> (Genesis 14:18–20)

The author of Hebrews points out that Melchizedek was a predecessor of Christ, the perfect priest-king:

> So also Christ did not exalt himself to be made a high priest, but was appointed by him who said to him,
> "You are my Son,
> today I have begotten you";
> as he says also in another place,
> "You are a priest for ever,
> according to the order of Melchizedek."
> In the days of his flesh, Jesus offered up prayers and supplications, with loud cries and tears, to him who was able to save him from death, and he was heard for his godly fear. Although he was a Son, he learned obedience through what he suffered; and being made perfect he became the source of eternal salvation to all who obey him, being designated by God a high priest according to the order of Melchizedek.
> (Hebrews 5:5–10)

The Passover sacrifice also prefigures the sacrifice of Christ. The Israelites sacrificed a lamb, whose blood spared them when the angel of death came for the firstborn of the Egyptians; the sacrifice of Christ on the cross defeated death forever. This is the sacrifice that is made present to us every time the Mass is offered (see question 6, Why is the Mass a sacrifice?).

During the Exodus the Israelites were in danger of starving in the desert until God gave them bread from heaven to eat.

> And when the dew had gone up, there was on the face of the wilderness a fine, flake-like thing, fine as hoarfrost on the ground. When the sons of Israel saw it, they said to one another, "What is it?" For they did not know what it was. And Moses said to them, "It is the bread which the Lord has given you to eat."...
>
> ...And Moses said, "This is what the Lord has commanded: 'Let an omer of it be kept throughout your generations, that they may see the bread with which I fed you in the wilderness, when I brought you out of the land of Egypt.'" And Moses said to Aaron, "Take a jar, and put an omer of manna in it, and place it before the Lord, to be kept throughout your generations." As the Lord commanded Moses, so Aaron placed it before the testimony, to be kept. And the sons of Israel ate the manna forty years, till they came to a habitable land; they ate the manna, till they came to the border of the land of Canaan. (Exodus 16:14–15, 32–35)

The manna that the Israelites gathered in the desert was a pale shadow of the Eucharist, as Christ told his followers when they asked him for a sign:

> So they said to him, "Then what sign do you do, that we may see, and believe you? What work do you perform? Our fathers ate the manna in the wilderness; as it is written, 'He gave them bread from heaven to eat.'" Jesus then said to them, "Truly, truly, I say to you, it was not Moses who gave you the bread from heaven; my Father gives you the true bread from heaven. For the bread of God is that which comes down from heaven, and gives life to the world." They said to him, "Lord, give us this bread always."
>
> Jesus said to them, "I am the bread of life; he who comes to me shall not hunger, and he who believes in me shall never thirst." (John 6:30–35)

In the tabernacle, and later the temple, where God met his people Israel, there was a table on which the "bread of the Presence" was always set before God (see Exodus 25:30). The bread represented the presence of God in the temple, prefiguring the bread of the Eucharist, which is God actually present in our churches. Only priests could eat the bread of the Presence.

When the Israelites gathered their first harvest in the Promised Land, they were instructed to bring an offering of wheat and wine to the altar of the Lord—and at the same time, they would sacrifice a lamb (see Leviticus 23:10–14). From then on they were to make the same offering every year. A Christian can hardly help seeing the offering of bread and wine *plus a lamb* as a symbolic precursor of what is offered in reality on our altars at every Mass.

The "sacrifice of thanksgiving"—in Hebrew, *todah*—often mentioned in the psalms (see Psalm 50; 116) is also an important precursor of the Mass. One common Greek translation of *todah* was *eucharistia,* from which we get our word *Eucharist.*

The prophet Malachi speaks for the Lord, telling Israel that the Lord has no pleasure in sacrifices that are offered with an impure heart:

> Oh, that there were one among you who would shut the doors, that you might not kindle fire upon my altar in vain! I have no pleasure in you, says the LORD of hosts, and I will not accept an offering from your hand. For from the rising of the sun to its setting my name is great among the nations, and in every place incense is offered to my name, and a pure offering; for my name is great among the nations, says the LORD of hosts. But you profane it when you say that the LORD's table is polluted, and the food for it may be despised. (Malachi 1:10–12)

Malachi says that the Lord's name is "great among the nations" all over the earth—from east to west—and the nations all offer pure sacrifices to the name of the Lord. Now, when Malachi wrote, that was not yet true. The name of the Lord was hardly known beyond a small part of the Middle East, and Israel was offering impure, grudging sacrifices. But a Christian sees a prophecy of the Mass in those words: The Mass really is a "pure offering" made from the rising of the sun to its setting, all over the world. The old sacrificial cult of Israel has passed away, but the real worship of God continues in every nation, wherever there is a Catholic altar.

20. What are the Jewish roots of the Christian ritual?

The Mass is the fulfillment of many of the Israelite rituals of the Old Testament. The Passover is probably the most important of these. The Last Supper was a Passover meal. For Christians it was the last Passover meal, because it fulfills the Passover.

The annual Passover celebration was a reenactment of God's redemption of his people. It commemorated the last plague of Egypt, when the angel of death took the firstborn sons of the Egyptians but passed over the sons of Israelites who had sacrificed a lamb and marked their doors with its blood. The Passover also celebrated the Exodus that followed, when God led his people out of slavery in Egypt and gave them the law by which they would live as a nation—a nation free from enslavement to idol worshippers and free to worship the true God.

Every year after that the Israelites were to sacrifice a lamb the way they had done at the first Passover, and they would eat unleavened bread to remember the haste with which they left their bondage in Egypt. From one generation to the next, the people would pass down the story of how God had redeemed them, and each new generation would experience something of what that redemption was like. (See question 48, Why does the Church use unleavened bread? for more about the connection of the Mass to the Passover.)

Scriptural and Historic Roots

Our Mass makes our own redemption present to us but, unlike the Passover, in a real and complete way. The sacrifice of Jesus Christ on the cross completed the work of redemption that had begun at the moment of our first sin. The Exodus was a big part of the story of redemption, but it was only a part. It released only one small group of people from their physical slavery. It did not release them from their bondage to sin, and it did not release the rest of the nations of the world from anything.

Sin offerings were also an important part of Israelite ritual. There were offerings prescribed for even trivial sins, and the rituals were detailed precisely in the Law. If you sinned by making a thoughtless oath, for example, or by accidentally touching something unclean, when you realized you'd sinned, you owed a sin offering.

> When a man is guilty in any of these, he shall confess the sin he has committed, and he shall bring his guilt offering to the LORD for the sin which he has committed, a female from the flock, a lamb or a goat, for a sin offering; and the priest shall make atonement for him for his sin.
>
> But if he cannot afford a lamb, then he shall bring, as his guilt offering to the LORD for the sin which he has committed, two turtledoves or two young pigeons, one for a sin offering and the other for a burnt offering. He shall bring them to the priest, who shall offer first the one for the sin offering; he shall wring its head from its neck, but shall not sever it, and he shall sprinkle some of the blood of the sin offering on the

> side of the altar, while the rest of the blood shall be drained out at the base of the altar; it is a sin offering. Then he shall offer the second for a burnt offering according to the ordinance; and the priest shall make atonement for him for the sin which he has committed, and he shall be forgiven. (Leviticus 5:5–10)

This ritual did not overcome sin. It forgave one sin of the past; it could not defeat sin itself. Only the sacrifice of Christ on the cross could release anyone from sin. This is the sacrifice that is present to us at every Mass.

The "sacrifice of thanksgiving," which is prescribed in Leviticus but not mentioned again till the time of David (see Leviticus 22:29–30), is another important precursor of our Mass. Our word *Eucharist*, in fact, comes from the Greek word that was often used as a translation for "sacrifice of thanksgiving."

> What shall I render to the LORD
>   for all his bounty to me?
> I will lift up the chalice of salvation
>   and call on the name of the LORD,
> I will pay my vows to the LORD
>   in the presence of all his people.
> Precious in the sight of the Lord
>   is the death of his saints.
> O LORD, I am your servant;
>   I am your servant, the son of your handmaid.
>   You have loosed my bonds.
> I will offer to you the sacrifice of thanksgiving
>   and call on the name of the LORD.

> I will pay my vows to the LORD
> in the presence of all his people,
> in the courts of the house of the LORD,
> in your midst, O Jerusalem.
> Praise the LORD! (Psalm 116:12–19)

All these sacrifices come together in our Mass because the sacrifice of Christ on the cross fulfilled all the sacrifices of the Old Testament. Christians no longer sacrifice animals or grain, because we know that the sacrifice of Christ is complete—one perfect sacrifice for all time.

Finally, our Liturgy of the Word—in which we hear the Scripture readings and the homily and say the prayers for everyone in need—seems to be based on the synagogue liturgy that was current at the time of Christ. In the synagogue—as we can see in numerous New Testament passages—the Scriptures were read by a lector, and then there was a kind of homily or interpretation, often by a visiting guest. We see this in Acts, for example, when Paul and his friends visit the synagogue of Antioch in Pisidia: "And on the sabbath day they went into the synagogue and sat down. After the reading of the law and the prophets, the rulers of the synagogue sent to them, saying, 'Brethren, if you have any word of exhortation for the people, say it'" (Acts 13:14–15).

And in Luke, Jesus himself, visiting the synagogue at Nazareth, is asked to read and interpret the Scripture for the day:

> And he came to Nazareth, where he had been brought up; and he went to the synagogue, as was his custom,

on the sabbath day. And he stood up to read; and there was given to him the book of the prophet Isaiah. He opened the book and found the place where it was written,

"The Spirit of the Lord is upon me,
because he has anointed me to preach good news to   the poor.
He has sent me to proclaim release to the captives
and recovering of sight to the blind,
to set at liberty those who are oppressed,
to proclaim the acceptable year of the Lord."

And he closed the book, and gave it back to the attendant, and sat down; and the eyes of all in the synagogue were fixed on him. And he began to say to them, "Today this Scripture has been fulfilled in your hearing." And all spoke well of him, and wondered at the gracious words which proceeded out of his mouth; and they said, "Is not this Joseph's son?" (Luke 4:16–22)

What we see from all these comparisons, then, is that Christian worship was a continuation of Jewish worship. This is no surprise. The early Christians never thought they were starting a new religion. They believed they were practicing the religion of Abraham, of Moses, of David—but now with the knowledge that they were living in the time of the Messiah.

21. Where does the Mass appear in the New Testament?
All four Gospels tell us about the Last Supper, which was the first Mass. There Jesus shared his body and blood with

his disciples and told them to continue the celebration he had taught them.

That meal was itself a preparation for the sacrifice of Christ on the cross, which is also in all four Gospels. What the Roman authorities saw as the execution of a common criminal was actually the sacrifice of the Lamb of God, which is made present to us every time the Eucharist is offered on our altars.

The story of Christ's appearance on the road to Emmaus seems to prefigure the Mass that we know today. Two of Christ's followers who haven't yet heard that he has risen from the dead meet him on the road to Emmaus, but they don't recognize him. As they walk along he begins to explain everything that has happened to him in light of the Old Testament:

> And beginning with Moses and all the prophets, he interpreted to them in all the Scriptures the things concerning himself.
>
> So they drew near to the village to which they were going. He appeared to be going further, but they constrained him, saying, "Stay with us, for it is toward evening and the day is now far spent." So he went in to stay with them. When he was at table with them, he took the bread and blessed and broke it, and gave it to them. And their eyes were opened and they recognized him; and he vanished out of their sight. (Luke 24:27–31)

This looks very much like our Mass today. First we hear the Scriptures, and the priest explains them to us. Then we have the breaking of the bread, and at that moment we recognize Christ's real presence among us in the bread and wine.

After that, the New Testament tells us, the early Christians faithfully followed the instructions Christ had given at the Last Supper. The Acts of the Apostles tells us that the very earliest Christians "held steadfastly to the apostles' teaching and fellowship, to the breaking of the bread and to the prayers" (Acts 2:42). From the very beginning "the breaking of bread" was the ceremony that defined Christian practice.

St. Paul reminded the Corinthians of what they had heard of the Last Supper, leaving us a summary that we still use in our Masses today:

> For I received from the Lord what I also delivered to you, that the Lord Jesus on the night when he was betrayed took bread, and when he had given thanks, he broke it, and said, "This is my body which is for you. Do this in remembrance of me." In the same way also the chalice, after supper, saying, "This chalice is the new covenant in my blood. Do this, as often as you drink it, in remembrance of me." For as often as you eat this bread and drink the chalice, you proclaim the Lord's death until he comes. (1 Corinthians 11:23–26)

St. Paul brings this up when reprimanding the Corinthians for not taking the Mass seriously enough. They seem to regard it as a kind of dinner party: "For in eating, each one goes ahead with his own meal, and one is hungry and another is drunk" (1 Corinthians 11:21). But our meal together is not for filling the stomach, Paul says. You have houses to eat in if you're hungry.

This little glimpse of the Corinthian church shows us both that the early Christians were celebrating the Mass as their central ceremony and that they were still refining their practice.

22. How did Jesus prepare his followers for the institution of the Mass?

It was a hard thing Jesus had to teach his followers, and they couldn't understand it all at once. Jesus was not just going to be a teacher or a leader: He was going to be a sacrifice. In fact, he was going to be *the* sacrifice, the end of all sacrifices, the one that would finally defeat sin. And somehow his followers were going to participate in that sacrifice.

St. John tells us that the sacrificial imagery was obvious from the beginning of Jesus' career. When John the Baptist saw Jesus coming toward him, he announced in a loud voice, "Behold, the Lamb of God, who takes away the sin of the world!" (John 1:29). He shouted, "Behold, the Lamb of God!" again the next day (John 1:36).

What did he mean by that? To an Israelite a "lamb" would naturally suggest a sacrificial animal. But if there were any doubt, John dispels it with the words "who takes away the sin of the world." What takes away sin is a sacrifice—a sin offering. Anyone who heard John speak would have known that right away. Nevertheless, they would almost certainly have been puzzled. The idea of a wandering teacher as a sin offering probably didn't make much sense to them. They had to see more to begin to understand.

St. John goes on to tell us that, after the feeding of the multitude, some of the people who had been following Jesus asked him for a sign:

So they said to him, "Then what sign do you do, that we may see, and believe you? What work do you perform? Our fathers ate the manna in the wilderness; as it is written, 'He gave them bread from heaven to eat.'" Jesus then said to them, "Truly, truly, I say to you, it was not Moses who gave you the bread from heaven; my Father gives you the true bread from heaven. For the bread of God is that which comes down from heaven, and gives life to the world." They said to him, "Lord, give us this bread always."

Jesus said to them, "I am the bread of life; he who comes to me shall not hunger, and he who believes in me shall never thirst. But I said to you that you have seen me and yet do not believe. All that the Father gives me will come to me; and him who comes to me I will not cast out. For I have come down from heaven, not to do my own will, but the will of him who sent me; and this is the will of him who sent me, that I should lose nothing of all that he has given me, but raise it up at the last day. For this is the will of my Father, that every one who sees the Son and believes in him should have eternal life; and I will raise him up at the last day." (John 6:30–40)

Many of the people who heard what Jesus said were appalled when he called himself "the bread of life." But instead of backing off, Jesus made it even harder for them. Knowing that they were grumbling, he went on to be much more explicit:

"I am the bread of life. Your fathers ate the manna in

> the wilderness, and they died. This is the bread which comes down from heaven, that a man may eat of it and not die. I am the living bread which came down from heaven; if any one eats of this bread, he will live for ever; and the bread which I shall give for the life of the world is my flesh."
>
> The Jews then disputed among themselves, saying, "How can this man give us his flesh to eat?" So Jesus said to them, "Truly, truly, I say to you, unless you eat the flesh of the Son of man and drink his blood, you have no life in you; he who eats my flesh and drinks my blood has eternal life, and I will raise him up at the last day. For my flesh is food indeed, and my blood is drink indeed. He who eats my flesh and drinks my blood abides in me, and I in him. As the living Father sent me, and I live because of the Father, so he who eats me will live because of me. This is the bread which came down from heaven, not such as the fathers ate and died; he who eats this bread will live for ever." This he said in the synagogue, as he taught at Capernaum.
>
> Many of his disciples, when they heard it, said, "This is a hard saying; who can listen to it?" (John 6:48–60)

After this, many who had been following Jesus left him. It's easy to see why if we think about it. What kind of madness is this? Unless we eat his flesh (the Greek verb for "eat" is shockingly graphic; it means something like "gnaw on") and drink his blood, we have no life? We came to learn from him, not to eat him!

The ones who did stay didn't really understand what Jesus meant either. But they put their faith first.

"Jesus said to the Twelve, 'Will you also go away?' Simon Peter answered him, 'Lord, to whom shall we go? You have the words of eternal life; and we have believed, and have come to know, that you are the Holy One of God'" (John 6:67–69).

23. Why do the accounts of the first Mass differ from book to book?

Each Gospel writer emphasized what he thought his audience needed to hear. Matthew probably wrote for Jewish Christians; Mark told what he had learned from Peter; Luke wrote for gentiles who might be unfamiliar with Jewish customs; and John wrote later to fill in and elaborate on what the others had told. Paul also wrote an account of the Last Supper to summarize what the Corinthians should have remembered about what they had been taught.

The heart of each account (except John's) is the words of institution, as we call them, in which Jesus gives his disciples the bread and wine and tells them they are his body and blood. We can start with Matthew's version:

> Now as they were eating, Jesus took bread, and blessed, and broke it, and gave it to the disciples and said, "Take, eat; this is my body."
>
> And he took a chalice, and when he had given thanks he gave it to them, saying, "Drink of it, all of you; for this is my blood of the covenant, which is poured out for many for the forgiveness of sins. I tell you I shall not drink again of this fruit of the vine until that day when I drink it new with you in my Father's kingdom." (Matthew 26:26–29)

St. Mark's account is very similar to Matthew's; the differences are small enough that many scholars think the two accounts come from the same source.

> And as they were eating, he took bread, and blessed, and broke it, and gave it to them, and said, "Take; this is my body." And he took a chalice, and when he had given thanks he gave it to them, and they all drank of it. And he said to them, "This is my blood of the covenant, which is poured out for many. Truly, I say to you, I shall not drink again of the fruit of the vine until that day when I drink it new in the kingdom of God." (Mark 14: 22–25)

St. Luke gives us a slightly more detailed description, and he seems to have the cup passed around twice:

> And when the hour came, he sat at table, and the apostles with him. And he said to them, "I have earnestly desired to eat this Passover with you before I suffer; for I tell you I shall not eat it until it is fulfilled in the kingdom of God." And he took a chalice, and when he had given thanks he said, "Take this, and divide it among yourselves; for I tell you that from now on I shall not drink of the fruit of the vine until the kingdom of God comes." And he took bread, and when he had given thanks he broke it and gave it to them, saying, "This is my body which is given for you. Do this in remembrance of me." And likewise the chalice after supper, saying, "This chalice which is poured out for you is the new covenant in my blood."

(Luke 22:14–20)

Alone among the Gospel writers, John leaves out the words of institution. His Gospel seems designed to fill in the gaps left by the other narratives, so it's not surprising that John instead gives us a long account of what Jesus revealed to his disciples at the end of the meal (see John 13—17).

Finally we have St. Paul's version (which we've seen once before), which matches what we hear from the three synoptic Gospels fairly closely:

> For I received from the Lord what I also delivered to you, that the Lord Jesus on the night when he was betrayed took bread, and when he had given thanks, he broke it, and said, "This is my body which is for you. Do this in remembrance of me." In the same way also the chalice, after supper, saying, "This chalice is the new covenant in my blood. Do this, as often as you drink it, in remembrance of me." For as often as you eat this bread and drink the chalice, you proclaim the Lord's death until he comes. (1 Corinthians 11:23–26)

Paul's account may well be the first one to have been written down, but what he tells us makes it obvious that he was only repeating what the Corinthians had already heard. Paul says he received it directly from the Lord and taught it to the Corinthians; he repeats it here not to tell them something new but to remind them of what they already know and to make them think about whether they've been behaving well at their shared meals.

As we might expect then, the differences are in details,

not in the outline of the story. The differences are exactly what you would expect from multiple witnesses, some reporting at second hand, describing a real event that had happened in the recent past.

The one difference that causes the most debate is an apparent difference in dates. In Luke the Last Supper is the main Passover meal, eaten on the day when the Passover lamb was sacrificed (see Luke 22:7–8). In John Jesus was crucified on the day the Passover lamb was sacrificed (see John 19:14–15). Many theories have been proposed to harmonize these two dates, including the possibility that one of them is calculated according to one of the alternative calendars used by some Jewish sects who didn't accept the official temple calculation.

But it's probably best to say that we just don't know. Both Luke and John are making the same point by noting the day, though with slightly different emphases. Both see Jesus as the perfect Passover lamb. Luke stresses the continuity of the Christian Mass with the Passover sacrifice. John stresses Jesus' death on the cross as the perfect Passover sacrifice.

24. How do we know that Jesus intended the Church to continue offering the Mass?

His instructions are simple and specific: "Do this in remembrance of me" (Luke 22:19). The people who knew him best—his apostles—followed those instructions, as we know from the Acts of the Apostles. Right after the coming of the Holy Spirit at Pentecost, Acts tells us, three thousand new Christians were baptized. "And they held steadfastly to the apostles' teaching and fellowship, to the breaking of the bread and to the prayers" (Acts 2:42).

"The breaking of bread" was the characteristic celebration that set the Christians apart from other Jews. While the temple still existed, the Christians worshiped there along with everyone else, but they had their own Masses in private homes: "And day by day, attending the temple together and breaking bread in their homes, they partook of food with glad and generous hearts, praising God and having favor with all the people. And the Lord added to their number day by day those who were being saved" (Acts 2:46–47).

So we have the witness of Scripture to tell us what Jesus' instructions were and to tell us that his apostles were following those instructions mere days after Jesus ascended into heaven. The tradition of the Mass is unbroken from the time of Christ to our own day.

25. Did the early Church—the persecuted, "underground" Church—celebrate the Mass? If so, how?

The Mass has been the center of Christian worship since the beginning, so the early Christians found ways to celebrate it even during the most intense persecutions. The celebration seems to have been very much like our current liturgy, although it's hard to establish some of the details for the very earliest celebrations, because the Christians of that time kept the Eucharist a secret from the unbaptized.

Often the Christians met at the tombs of the martyrs for morning prayers. They may have celebrated what we call the Liturgy of the Word there and then celebrated the Eucharist at someone's private house later on, or they may have just prayed at the tombs and then celebrated the whole

Scriptural and Historic Roots

Mass later in the day—it's not quite clear from the sources we have. One pagan governor who was also a famous writer, Pliny the Younger, mentions in a letter to the emperor that Christians gathered for prayers before dawn.[1]

St. Justin Martyr, who was writing in about the year 150, describes the Eucharist in terms we easily recognize:

> Then the president of the brethren is brought bread and a cup of wine mixed with water. Taking them, he gives praise and glory to the Father of the universe, through the name of the Son and of the Holy Spirit, and offers thanks at considerable length for our being counted worthy to receive these things at His hands. And when he has concluded the prayers and thanksgivings, all the people present express their assent by saying Amen, which means "so be it" in Hebrew.
>
> And when the president has given thanks, and all the people have expressed their assent, the ones we call deacons give to each of those present to partake of the bread and wine mixed with water over which the thanksgiving was pronounced [or more literally, that has been *eucharisted*], and they take some of it away to those who are absent.
>
> We call this food the Eucharist. No one is allowed to partake of it unless he believes that the things we teach are true, and has been washed with the baptism that is for the remission of sins and regeneration, and who lives the way Christ taught us to live.
>
> For we do not take them as common bread and common drink. But just as Jesus Christ our Saviour,

having been made flesh by the Word of God, had both flesh and blood for our salvation, in the same way have we been taught that the food that is blessed by the prayer of his word, and from which our blood and flesh by transmutation are nourished, is the flesh and blood of that Jesus who was made flesh.

For the apostles, in the memoirs composed by them, which are called Gospels, have told us what they were taught: that Jesus took bread, and when he had given thanks, said, "This do in remembrance of me; this is my body"; and that, after the same manner, having taken the cup and given thanks, he said, "This is my blood"; and gave it to them alone.[2]

A work known as *The Apostolic Tradition*, which comes to us from the early third century, gives a very complete account of the Eucharistic liturgy in the time when Christianity was still a persecuted underground sect. If you're familiar with the Mass of today, these ancient words are almost startlingly familiar:

Priest: The Lord be with you.
People: And with your spirit.
Priest: Lift up your hearts.
People: We lift them to the Lord.
Priest: Let us give thanks to the Lord.
People: It is right and just.

Then the priest goes on like this: We give you thanks, O God, through your beloved Son, whom in these last days you have sent to us as a Savior, and a Redeemer, and a Messenger of your will.

You sent him from heaven into the womb of the Virgin, and he became incarnate, and showed himself as your Son, born of the Holy Spirit and the Virgin.

To do your will, and to win you a holy people, he stretched out his hands in suffering, so that he might free those from suffering who believed in you.

When he was about to hand himself over to willing suffering so that he might destroy death, and break the chains of the devil, and stamp out hell, and shed light on the righteous, and establish the covenant, and show forth the resurrection, he took bread, and giving thanks to you said, "Take, eat; this is my body, which is broken for you."

Likewise he took the cup, saying, "This is my blood, which is shed for you. When you do this, do it in memory of me."

Therefore, remembering his death and resurrection, we offer you the bread and the cup, giving thanks to you that you have deemed us worthy to stand before you and minister to you.

And we pray that you will send your Holy Spirit on the offering of your holy Church, bringing together as one all who receive it, filled with the Holy Spirit to confirm their faith in truth, so that we may praise and glorify you through your Son Jesus Christ, through whom be glory and honor to you, Father and Son, with the Holy Spirit, in your holy Church, both now and throughout the ages. Amen.[3]

When the text says, "Then the priest goes on like this," it probably means that the exact words are up to the priest.

We have good evidence that, in those very early years, priests improvised the parts of the liturgy that didn't require public response. Of course, they had to keep within very strict limits. For example, this sample prayer includes an institution narrative (see question 92, What is the institution narrative?), and the priest who chose his own words would certainly have to include that. It wasn't long before the exact words were prescribed, which more easily kept the priests within the bounds of orthodoxy.

These examples show us not only that the early Christians celebrated the Mass but also that they celebrated it in a way that we would have recognized. The many centuries between them and us would bring gradual developments and changes, but the fundamentals were already in place in the Mass of the age of martyrs and heroes.

The Celebrant

26. Who may offer the Mass?

An ordained priest offers the Mass. That may be a bishop, an archbishop, or the pope himself, since they are, of course, all ordained priests. The priest who celebrates the Mass is called the *celebrant*. Sometimes there is more than one priest, in which case there is a main celebrant and concelebrants.

The priest actually represents Christ, and the sacrifice of the Mass is really offered by Christ, our great High Priest. Because there is only one sacrifice for all time, there is really only one Priest who offers it:

> The former priests were many in number, because they were prevented by death from continuing in office; but he holds his priesthood permanently, because he continues for ever. Consequently he is able for all time to save those who draw near to God through him, since he always lives to make intercession for them.

> For it was fitting that we should have such a high priest, holy, blameless, unstained, separated from sinners, exalted above the heavens. He has no need, like those high priests, to offer sacrifices daily, first for his own sins and then for those of the people; he did this once for all when he offered up himself. Indeed, the law appoints men in their weakness as high priests, but the word of the oath, which came later than the law, appoints a Son who has been made perfect for ever. (Hebrews 7:23–28)

Sometimes groups of Catholics live in an area where there is no resident priest. They still get together to worship on Sunday, but the worship service is not a Mass. Catholics in a situation like this treasure the occasional visits of a priest, because only then can the Mass be celebrated.

27. How did Jesus give our priests the power to change bread and wine into his body and blood?

When he told his disciples, "Do this in remembrance of me," Jesus gave them both a positive instruction and the means to accomplish it. These disciples became the first leaders of the Catholic Church, eventually appointing others to help them carry out their work; and their successors, the bishops, still exercise the responsibility of ordaining priests to serve at the altar of Christ.

Every priest receives the sacrament of holy orders, which gives him the spiritual power and authority that Christ gave to his disciples to offer the sacrifice of the Mass. By the power of the Holy Spirit, holy orders marks the priest with an indelible character. The priesthood is not just a job a man takes on for a period of time; he is a priest for life. Even if he does something so terribly wrong that the Church has to deprive him of his priestly authority, that indelible character stays with him.

28. What is a pontifical Mass?

A pontifical Mass is a Mass at which the celebrant is a bishop—which could also mean an archbishop or even the pope, who is bishop of Rome. There are certain extra ceremonies in the Mass when a bishop celebrates it, but the main body of the Mass is the same.

29. Is Mass with the pope or bishop "worth more" than Mass in my parish?

No. Every Mass is a miracle, and in every Mass we are brought into the precincts of heaven, no matter how humble our earthly surroundings. The same grace comes to us whether the celebrant is a newly ordained priest or the Holy Father.

For many Christians, however, a Mass celebrated by the pope or by a bishop is an intensely moving religious experience. If you visit Rome and see the pope celebrating Mass, you'll remember that Mass for the rest of your life. Experiences like that are good and important: They can reinforce our faith and give us a new enthusiasm that we carry home with us. In the same way a Mass in a Quonset hut is as much a miracle as a Mass in a Gothic cathedral—but there's nothing wrong with enjoying and being inspired by the beauty of the cathedral.

30. Does there have to be a congregation for there to be a Mass?

No. A priest marooned on a desert island could offer the Mass if he could find the bread and wine to do it. Even when no congregation is present, the sacrifice of Christ is the source of immeasurable good for the world. Masses are often offered for particular intentions without a congregation.

31. What are the vestments the priest wears?

The *alb* is the long white tunic that the priest wears—in fact, the word *alb* comes from the Latin *album*, meaning "white." It may be ornamented a little with embroidery around the edges, but otherwise it's plain white, to symbolize someone who's been washed clean by God's grace. Priests aren't the only ones who wear albs; anyone who is visibly serving at Mass may wear one if that's the customary practice in the parish, including the choir and the altar servers.

The *cincture* is the rope tied like a belt around the priest's waist. Practically speaking it holds the alb against his body; symbolically it represents chastity.

The *chasuble* is the priest's outer garment, which identifies him right away as a priest celebrating the Mass. It is usually in the liturgical color of the day (see question 33, What do the colors of the vestments mean?). It can be decorated, often with a cross on the back.

The *stole* is something like a long scarf worn by a priest over his alb and under his chasuble but by a bishop over his chasuble. Like the chasuble, it's in the liturgical color of the day. There is a cross in the very center of the stole, where it hangs from the priest's neck. Deacons also wear stoles; a deacon's stole crosses from his left shoulder to his right side, whereas a priest's or bishop's stole hangs straight down.

The *amice* is not usually obvious to people in the congregation. It's a linen rectangle worn over the neck and under the alb. Originally it probably had the humble and practical purpose of keeping the outer vestments from getting soiled. Now when it is used, it is a symbol of the "helmet of salvation" (Ephesians 5:17).

32. Why does the priest wear vestments?

The priest wears vestments for the same reason a policeman wears a badge, a king wears a crown, and a bride wears a wedding gown. These are all visible symbols that tell us immediately who the person is and what he's doing.

The vestments of our priests and bishops actually come from ancient times. Some of them hark back to the garments of the Israelite priests who served in the Jerusalem temple. Other items represent what a well-dressed Roman would put on for his Sunday best; the chasuble, for example, was a traveling cloak. The apostles wore similar clothes when they preached the gospel to the earliest Christians.

As fashions changed the Church kept these distinctive clothes as symbols of her ancient tradition and authority—and of the dignity, solemnity, and beauty of the priestly office. The vestments have changed in minor ways over the centuries, but in their fundamental shape and use, they're still what the ancients wore.

33. What do the colors of the vestments mean?

Every day in the Church calendar is assigned a particular symbolic color, and the priest's chasuble and stole for the day, and the altar decorations as well, will usually be in that color.

White, a symbol of purity, is used for Christmas, Easter, Masses in honor of the Blessed Virgin Mary, most funerals, and a number of other festivals.

Red, a symbol of love, is used for Passion (or Palm) Sunday, Good Friday, Pentecost, and feasts of martyrs.

Purple, a symbol of penance, is used for Advent and Lent, which are both times of repentance.

Rose, a symbol of joy, is used for Gaudete Sunday and Laetare Sunday, which are days of joy midway through the penitential seasons of Advent and Lent.

In Ordinary Time, when there is no other particular celebration, the color is *green*, which is a symbol of hope.

For certain special occasions, such as Christmas and Easter, the priest may also choose to wear *gold*. Sometimes (though not very often anymore) *black* vestments are used for funerals; more often *white* is used.

OBLIGATION AND OPPORTUNITY

34. How often must I go to Mass?

Mass is required every Sunday (in many parishes you can attend a Saturday evening "vigil Mass" instead). You also need to go to Mass on certain important festivals, which we call "holy days of obligation." Once again, Mass is often offered on the evening before these holy days, and the evening Mass fulfills the obligation.

The bishops of a particular country or area decide which days are holy days of obligation. In the United States these are so designated:

- January 1: The Solemnity of Mary, Mother of God
- Thursday of the Sixth Week of Easter: The Solemnity of the Ascension (though some dioceses celebrate the Ascension on the following Sunday)
- August 15: The Solemnity of the Assumption of the Blessed Virgin Mary
- November 1: The Solemnity of All Saints

- December 8: The Solemnity of the Immaculate Conception
- December 25: The Solemnity of the Nativity of Our Lord Jesus Christ

In rare emergencies the bishop of your diocese may grant a "dispensation" from the obligation to attend Mass—for example, when weather conditions make it dangerous to travel. Illness also relieves you of the obligation. Some bishops will dispense of the obligation if the holy day falls on a Saturday or a Monday. But the obligation to attend Mass on holy days should be taken seriously.

On the other hand, thinking of Mass as an obligation is really a backward way of looking at it. Going to Mass is an extraordinary privilege. Instead of trying to decide when you *have* to go, why not go as often as you can? Most parishes have Masses every day, and you may find that the Mass is the perfect way to start your morning.

35. Why does the Church require us to go to Mass on Sunday?

One of the Ten Commandments warns us to remember the Sabbath day:

> Remember the sabbath day, to keep it holy. Six days you shall labor, and do all your work; but the seventh day is a sabbath to the LORD your God; in it you shall not do any work, you, or your son, or your daughter, your manservant, or your maidservant, or your cattle, or the sojourner who is within your gates; for in six days the Lord made heaven and earth, the sea, and all

that is in them, and rested the seventh day; therefore the LORD blessed the sabbath day and hallowed it. (Exodus 20:8–11)

The Sabbath was the seventh day of the week—the day we call Saturday. As the commandment says, the Israelites were not to do any kind of work on the Sabbath. Even their domestic animals had to be allowed to rest. By New Testament times the Pharisees had built up all kinds of rules about what could and could not be done on the Sabbath. They often debated Jesus on the subject.

One sabbath [Jesus] was going through the grainfields; and as they made their way his disciples began to pluck heads of grain. And the Pharisees said to him, "Look, why are they doing what is not lawful on the sabbath?" And he said to them, "Have you never read what David did, when he was in need and was hungry, he and those who were with him: how he entered the house of God, when Abiathar was high priest, and ate the showbread, which it is not lawful for any but the priests to eat, and also gave it to those who were with him?" And he said to them, "The sabbath was made for man, not man for the sabbath; so the Son of man is lord even of the sabbath." (Mark 2:23–28)

It's important to notice that Jesus didn't object to the Sabbath itself. Observing it was one of the commandments. What he objected to was the legalism that forgot the point of the Sabbath. It was supposed to be a day of rest, when people could stop working and pay attention to higher things. It was not supposed to be a painful labor in its own right. The *Catechism of the Catholic Church* strikingly and even scandalously calls the Sabbath "a day of protest against the servitude of work and the worship of money" (*CCC*, #2172). It liberates us, if only for one day out of seven, from slavery to mundane concerns and frees us to look upward toward God.

So Jesus never abrogated the commandment to observe the Sabbath. But Christians take their day of rest on the Lord's Day (as it's been called since New Testament times), Sunday, the day Jesus Christ rose from the dead. Christ's resurrection is the historical fact at the center of Christian faith. The resurrection of Christ on Sunday is the fulfillment of the Sabbath: It foretells our own eternal rest with Christ in heaven.

Part of that rest is the spiritual refreshment of the Mass. Our Sunday obligation gives us two things we desperately need and that we tend not to leave time for if we're left to ourselves: It gives us rest, and it gives us close contact with the divine. It reminds us about God's love and the purpose of our lives and provides us with the opportunity to give God fitting worship.

Especially in modern secular society, the temptation is to work without ceasing—or to cause others to work constantly for us. But we are more than machines for performing work. We are God's children, with not only a right but an obligation to make ourselves better and to help others around us become better.

The obligation to go to Mass on Sunday takes us out of the cycle of endless labor. It forces us to make room in our lives for joy, whether we like it or not! We spend an hour a week remembering that there is something beyond our incessant pursuit of material things.

The Church teaches us to avoid doing anything on Sunday that would interfere with the rest we need for our bodies and our minds—the rest that enables us to order and direct our lives to God. Sometimes it's not possible to avoid working on Sunday, but we have to be sure we're working because of a genuine need rather than a mere habit or inclination. This is the principle Jesus laid down for us: Necessity overcomes the Sabbath obligation, as necessity made it reasonable for David and his men to eat the bread of the presence.

But even if we do work on Sunday out of serious necessity, we need to make sure we do what we can to live in a way that acknowledges the Lord's Day. We need to find some time when we can go to Mass, which in most places is not difficult.

Besides every Sunday, there are certain other days throughout the year when the Church requires us to attend Mass and rest from "works and activities" that "could impede such a sanctification of these days" (*CCC*, #2042). These "holy days of obligation" are important feasts in the Church calendar. (See question 34, How often must I go to Mass?)

For both Sundays and the other holy days, it's possible to fulfill your obligation by going to Mass the evening before the day, if a Mass is offered then in your parish. Because the Church takes these obligations very seriously, most parishes go out of their way to make it easy to comply with them.

36. Can I satisfy the Sunday obligation by going to Vespers instead of Mass?

No. That doesn't mean it's not good to go to a Vespers service if there's one in your parish. In fact, it's a very good thing to take part in the services the Church offers at different times of the day, because it builds worship into the rhythm of the day. But you do have to go to Mass on Sunday, or on Saturday evening if your parish has a Mass then (see question 35, Why does the Church require us to go to Mass on Sunday?).

37. What does it mean to offer the Mass for a particular "intention"?

Offering the Mass for a particular intention is an ancient Catholic custom. It's a way of directing the Church's most powerful form of prayer toward some good for which we earnestly desire to pray. The Mass can be offered for someone who needs help, for peace between nations, or for any other good intention that is pleasing to God and upholds his glory. It cannot be offered, of course, for evil or worthless intentions.

If you look at the Sunday bulletin of a typical Catholic parish, you'll often see the names of people, living or deceased, or particular concerns listed beside the schedule of Masses. These are the intentions for which the Masses are being offered to God. You can request that a Mass be offered for your own particular intention; usually people give a donation with such requests.

If you attend a Mass offered for a particular intention, you should do your best to offer your own prayers for the same intention. That way the whole congregation, united in one powerful body by Holy Communion, will be offering the same prayers.

38. Why do Catholics offer Masses for the dead?

Christians know that death is not the end of life but the real beginning. Freed from the imperfections of earthly existence, the dead are *more* alive than we are. They are with us, and we still live with them in love.

St. John tells us about the heavenly Jerusalem in Revelation. It is more beautiful, more glorious, than we can imagine. "But nothing unclean shall enter it," he adds (Revelation 21:27). So the Catholic Church tells us that there is a purification after death. St. Paul hints at it when he writes to the Corinthians about building on the foundation of Christ:

> For no other foundation can any one lay than that which is laid, which is Jesus Christ. Now if any one builds on the foundation with gold, silver, precious stones, wood, hay, straw—each man's work will become manifest; for the Day will disclose it, because it will be revealed with fire, and the fire will test what sort of work each one has done. If the work which any man has built on the foundation survives, he will receive a reward. If any man's work is burned up, he will suffer loss, though he himself will be saved, but only as through fire. (1 Corinthians 3:11–15)

In metalworking, fire burns off the impurities, leaving only the pure metal. St. Paul sees the same sort of thing happening on the Day of the Lord. Whoever has built on the foundation of Jesus Christ will be saved, but first the "fire" will purify us. This purification is what we call purgatory. There all our impurities are cleaned away, and we are made ready to enter heaven. We offer Masses for the dead as a way of speeding that purification for them.

Offering sacrifices for someone else is certainly no new idea. It was common practice in Old Testament times.

> There was a man in the land of Uz, whose name was Job; and that man was blameless and upright, one who feared God, and turned away from evil.... His sons used to go and hold a feast in the house of each on his day; and they would send and invite their three sisters to eat and drink with them. And when the days of the feast had run their course, Job would send and sanctify them, and he would rise early in the morning and offer burnt offerings according to the number of them all; for Job said, "It may be that my sons have sinned, and cursed God in their hearts." Thus Job did continually. (Job 1:1, 4–5)

Job, who was "blameless and upright," offered sacrifices for his sons *just in case*. Offering sacrifice for another was something a good person would be expected to do.

If indeed the dead are still with us, and even more alive than we are, then it would be shameful neglect not to pray and make offerings for them as much as for the living. The second book of Maccabees tells us how Judas Maccabeus offered prayers and sacrifices for his dead soldiers when he discovered that they had sinned.

> Judas and his men went to take up the bodies of the

fallen and to bring them back to lie with their kinsmen in the sepulchers of their fathers. Then under the tunic of every one of the dead they found sacred tokens of the idols of Jamnia, which the law forbids the Jews to wear. And it became clear to all that this was why these men had fallen. So they all blessed the ways of the Lord, the righteous Judge, who reveals the things that are hidden; and they turned to prayer, begging that the sin which had been committed might be wholly blotted out. And the noble Judas exhorted the people to keep themselves free from sin, for they had seen with their own eyes what had happened because of the sin of those who had fallen. He also took up a collection, man by man, to the amount of two thousand drachmas of silver, and sent it to Jerusalem to provide for a sin offering. In doing this he acted very well and honorably, taking account of the resurrection. For if he were not expecting that those who had fallen would rise again, it would have been superfluous and foolish to pray for the dead. But if he was looking to the splendid reward that is laid up for those who fall asleep in godliness, it was a holy and pious thought. Therefore he made atonement for the dead, that they might be delivered from their sin. (2 Maccabees 12:39–45)

Judas Maccabeus knew that the end of earthly life was not the end of life. His prayers could still do good for his friends.

It's worth knowing that the books of Maccabees don't appear in Protestant Bibles, so you won't win an argument with a Protestant by citing 2 Maccabees as Scripture. But the story proves unequivocally that sacrifices for the dead were normal Jewish practice in the time before Christ. Prayer for the dead remains a normal part of Jewish mourning today.

We Catholics pray and offer Masses both for the dead and for the living, and for exactly the same reasons. God hears and answers our prayers for others. And all who have ever lived are still living.

39. How does the Mass relate to the other sacraments?

All the other sacraments point toward the Mass, and the Mass in some sense includes all the other sacraments. Confession, for example, prepares us for our encounter with the Lord at Mass. Weddings and confirmations often take place within the Mass. Christians since the first generation have seen baptism as a necessary prerequisite to receiving Holy Communion at Mass. The anointing of the sick is often accompanied by Holy Communion in the form of *viaticum* (see question 65, What is *viaticum*?).

The Eucharist is the sacrament in which we are actually united in communion with God. All the other sacraments are in some way at the service of that communion, preparing us for it or helping us maintain it.

40. What is the relationship between the Mass and social justice?

The Mass is the fuel for social justice. When we meet at Mass, we're united in communion with Christ. We become one body, without distinctions between rich and poor or weak and strong. Every believer is equal at the Lord's table.

St. Paul was quite shocked to find the Corinthians violating this principle. It seems they had been celebrating the Eucharist by getting together to eat, but it was a meal at which each participant brought his or her own food. The rich stuffed themselves, and the poor went hungry.

> But in the following instructions I do not commend you, because when you come together it is not for the better but for the worse. For, in the first place, when you assemble as a Church, I hear that there are divisions among you; and I partly believe it, for there must be factions among you in order that those who are genuine among you may be recognized. When you meet together, it is not the Lord's supper that you eat. For in eating, each one goes ahead with his own meal, and one is hungry and another is drunk. What! Do you not have houses to eat and drink in? Or do you despise the Church of God and humiliate those who have nothing? What shall I say to you? Shall I commend you in this? No, I will not. (1 Corinthians 11:17–22)

St. Paul is very firm here: "It is not the Lord's supper that you eat" if you "humiliate those who have nothing." We must be truly united, sharing what we have and making no distinctions.

Nor can we leave that unity behind when we walk out of Mass. The Mass has to be life-changing, or we've missed the whole point of it. We have formed one body. Now when we see any of our brothers and sisters suffering injustice, we have to respond. We have to give what we have and remember that they are our equals. "So faith, hope, love abide, these three; but the greatest of these is love" (1 Corinthians 13:13).

41. How is the Mass like heaven?

When we're at Mass, we're participating in the joyous worship that goes on eternally in heaven. Obviously we can't know precisely what heaven is like—it's too wonderful, too glorious for our limited mortal comprehension. But Scripture gives us images to help us get some idea of what heaven is, especially in the Old Testament prophets and the New Testament book of Revelation. What we see in those images is our Christian liturgy, eternally celebrated in the heavenly court of the Father.

Many of the words of our liturgy come straight from those passages of Scripture. The *Sanctus*, or "Holy, Holy, Holy," is the hymn the seraphim sing at the throne of God (see question 91, What is the "Holy, Holy, Holy"?). We also recognize just before Communion these words of the angel from Revelation: "Blessed are those who are invited to the marriage supper of the Lamb" (Revelation 19:9). In the Mass we participate for the moment in that marriage supper of the Lamb that goes on eternally in heaven.

But the most important way the Mass is like heaven is not in the details of the liturgy. To be in heaven is to be with Christ, dwelling constantly in the presence of the living God. In the Mass we meet Christ face to face. In Holy Communion we are truly with Christ. When that happens we're in heaven, and no matter how unheavenly the rest of our earthly lives may be, we carry heaven with us into the world if we have the faith to see the truth of what we've just experienced.

Rites

42. Why do some Catholic churches celebrate the Eucharist in ways that are far different from the way I know?

The Catholic Church has more than a billion members, living on every inhabited continent. In the last two thousand years, many different liturgical traditions have grown up in different places. The liturgies all have the same basic elements, but they differ widely in the details.

Most Catholic churches in North America follow the tradition of the Latin rite, but many immigrant groups have kept their own traditions. Catholics from Eastern Europe, for example, may belong to a Byzantine rite church, which uses an ancient Eastern liturgy. There are also Maronite Christians, Syriac Christians, Malabar Christians, and many other groups who kept their old traditions when they settled in the New World. Though these congregations in America have their own rites, and some even their own bishops, they are still Catholic Christians, united with Rome in the one Catholic Church. And although their liturgies may seem very different at first glance, a closer and longer look will show that they all have the same essential parts.

Even within the Latin rite, there are variations. For example, parishes may use different Eucharistic Prayers, of which there are four (see question 88, What is the Eucharistic Prayer?). The musical tastes of parishes may be very different, reflecting the traditions of their congregations: You may hear a gigantic pipe organ at one church and a couple of guitars at another; or you may hear a full chorus, with a symphony orchestra, singing a Mass by Mozart or Beethoven. The Mass may be celebrated in Latin, English, Italian, German, Slovak, or some other language.

All these differences are part of the rich variety of traditions within the one tradition of the Church. The details can change in infinite ways, which is why the Mass has attracted the attention of great artists and composers. But the Mass is always the same—always the sacrifice of Jesus Christ, made really present before us on our altar.

43. What is the Latin Mass?

Latin is the official language of the Roman Catholic Church, and until relatively recently, Masses in the Western Church were always in Latin. The official rites of the liturgy are still promulgated in Latin but are then translated into the vernacular—English, French, Spanish, or another language. Priests have the freedom, however, to offer the Mass in Latin instead of the vernacular.

44. What is the Tridentine Mass or Extraordinary Form?

The Tridentine Mass—sometimes called the Traditional Latin Mass or the Extraordinary Form—follows the rites used in the West from ancient times up until the late 1960s. It preserves ancient Latin prayers and many beautiful and meaningful gestures, such as the people and priest together facing the East.

The ritual of this Mass was codified by the Council of Trent, held in the city of Trent or Trento in Italy. The Latin form of the name is *Tridentum*, and so the Mass promulgated there is called Tridentine. The name can be misleading. Though the council receives credit for standardizing the ritual of the Mass, many of the prayers had been in common use since the early centuries of Christianity.

The Tridentine Mass is also often referred to as the Extraordinary Form of the Mass, because it's not the form of the Mass ordinarily used in the Church today. From the 1970s onward the Church placed restrictions on the use of the Tridentine rites. In the year 2007, however, Pope Benedict XVI authorized a much wider use of the Tridentine Mass according to the 1962 missal.

Occasionally a "Traditional Latin Mass" is offered by groups that are separated from the Catholic Church. In recent years progress has been made toward reuniting with some of these schismatic groups.

45. Why do some Catholics like the Latin Mass so much?

Some people, of course, like the Latin Mass because they grew up with it. It just seems more like the Mass to them. There's nothing wrong with that. Sentimental attachments are good when they lead us toward the real object of our devotion. You might treasure a lock of hair given to you years ago by someone you loved—not because the hair was as important as the person, but because it has strong emotional associations with that person. In the same way, you might have a strong emotional attachment to the Latin Mass because it reminds you of the Mass as you first learned to love it.

The Tridentine Mass has its own kind of poetry and majesty that are different from the poetry and majesty of the Mass that succeeded it, and some younger Catholics who grew up with the current Mass love the older Mass just for its beauty.

There are good reasons for vernacular Masses, and North American bishops have concluded that it's best for people to have the Mass in a language they can understand. But the Holy Father has made it clear that there should be opportunities for people who love the Latin Mass to participate in it.

46. Why is Latin still the official language of the Mass in the Catholic Church?

The Church has been offering the Mass in Latin for centuries. The Latin Mass was originally the product of another movement to have the Mass in the vernacular. In the early years of Christianity, the Mass was usually in Greek because that was the language the apostles spoke. Every educated Roman knew Greek, but ordinary people in the western part of the Roman Empire spoke Latin. Eventually the Mass began to be offered in the language ordinary people could understand.

As the western half of the empire broke up, the Latin language quickly splintered into mutually unintelligible descendants like French, Romanian, Italian, and Spanish. But the Church in that part of the world kept the Mass in Latin. It was a force for unity: Europe might be broken into hundreds of squabbling duchies and principalities, but everywhere the Mass was the same. And at a time when literacy was rare and written culture was hanging by a thread, the Church insisted that her leaders should be able to read and understand the language of the great literature of the past.

Latin also gave the Church a useful neutrality. Far above the petty quarrels of dukes and princes, the Church did not take sides. The king of England might be warring against the king of France, but neither king could say that the Mass was in his language so God must be on his side.

As travel grew easier and the world opened up, Catholics found another reason to be grateful for the Latin Mass. Everywhere they went, from Indianapolis to Jakarta, the Mass was the same. You could step inside a local Catholic church and be right at home.

Though we usually see Masses in our own language today, Latin is still the official language of the Mass. Latin is a very precise language, partly because Catholic theologians have spent many centuries honing its theological terms to express very exact meanings. With the Latin version as the official wording of the Mass, there is one universal standard to which all vernacular translations can conform. So even though the Mass is in many different languages, it's always the same Mass.

47. Do non-Catholic churches also celebrate the Mass?

Orthodox churches celebrate the Mass, with a liturgy very similar to the Catholic liturgy. They usually use other terms for it, such as "Divine Liturgy."

Some Protestant churches celebrate a similar liturgy, and some Lutheran and Anglican congregations call it a Mass. To a Catholic, however, it isn't really the Mass. There must be a sacramentally ordained priesthood to celebrate the Mass, and Protestants don't accept ordination as a sacrament. They don't usually believe the same things we Catholics believe about the priesthood or about the Eucharist. Lutherans believe in the real presence (see question 10, What is the real presence?) but not in transubstantiation (see question 13, What is transubstantiation?). Most Anglicans also deny transubstantiation. These differences make it impossible for a Catholic to call Protestant services true "Masses," even if the Protestants call them that.

Properly Equipped

48. Why does the Church use unleavened bread?

Unleavened bread is one of the main features of the Passover. It commemorates the Israelites' hasty exit from Egypt: "And they baked unleavened cakes of the dough which they had brought out of Egypt, for it was not leavened, because they were thrust out of Egypt and could not tarry, neither had they prepared for themselves any provisions" (Exodus 12:39).

In memory of that Exodus, the Israelites were to celebrate the Passover for a week every year. During that week only unleavened bread was allowed.

> And when the LORD brings you into the land of the Canaanites, the Hittites, the Amorites, the Hivites, and the Jebusites, which he swore to your fathers to give you, a land flowing with milk and honey, you shall keep this service in this month. Seven days you shall eat unleavened bread, and on the seventh day there shall be a feast to the LORD. Unleavened bread shall be eaten for seven days; no leavened bread shall be

seen with you, and no leaven shall be seen with you in all your territory. And you shall tell your son on that day, "It is because of what the LORD did for me when I came out of Egypt." And it shall be to you as a sign on your hand and as a memorial between your eyes, that the law of the LORD may be in your mouth; for with a strong hand the LORD has brought you out of Egypt. (Exodus 13:5–9)

Jesus and his disciples were celebrating the Passover at the Last Supper. "And he said to them, 'I have earnestly desired to eat this Passover with you before I suffer; for I tell you I shall not eat it until it is fulfilled in the kingdom of God'" (Luke 22:15–16).

So we know that the bread used at the Last Supper was unleavened bread. Our Christian Eucharist follows the pattern laid down by Christ at that Passover meal. We repeat, as far as practical, the circumstances of Christ's meal with his disciples, including unleavened wheat bread.

49. May the priest use other types of bread?

The bread must be unleavened, and it must be made of wheat. It can't be leavened wheat bread, and it can't be unleavened bread mixed with other grains so much that we can no longer reasonably call it wheat bread. Communion wafers meet these requirements, which is why most parishes use them.

In theory there's nothing to prevent another kind of unleavened wheat bread from being used. But because it becomes the sacred Body of Christ, the priest has to be very careful not to lose crumbs of it when it is divided.

50. May a priest use gluten-free wheat bread for the sake of people who have celiac disease?

Not gluten-free, but low-gluten hosts can be used. Wheat is the essential matter; wheat flour with the gluten reduced can be substituted without invalidating the sacrament, but with no gluten at all, it's really not wheat bread anymore.

51. What if my body can't take any wheat at all?

If it's not possible to arrange for low-gluten bread for Communion, or if your body can't take even the tiny amount of gluten in a low-gluten wafer (ask your doctor), remember that Christ is completely present in both elements (see question 64, Is it better to receive Communion under both species? Do I receive "more" if I do?). Speak to the priest about receiving only from the chalice. Although it's unusual, canon law makes it clear that the priest can give you the Precious Blood alone if it's necessary. (This may require some preparation though, so be sure to speak to the priest well before Mass.)

Just as when the congregation receives only the consecrated Host, the Sacrament is no less valid if you receive only the Sacred Blood. Don't abstain from Communion just because you can't digest wheat. Christ wants to come to you, and he certainly won't turn you away.

52. What are the vessels used in the Mass?

There are special vessels with particular names for the Eucharist. Like the priests' vestments, these vessels actually come from daily life in Roman times, they were part of the ordinary table setting at a formal dinner. Over time vessels for the Mass were set aside as sacred and were made more beautiful. They've been developed for the Church's particular requirements, but they would still be recognizable to a well-bred Roman citizen.

The vessels we use at Mass are usually made of gold or silver, and there are both practical and symbolic reasons for that choice. Symbolically, of course, we honor Christ our Lord by choosing the most precious things we have for the vessels in which he will make himself present. Practically we need vessels that will not break and that will stand up to long use, and precious metals meet both requirements.

The vessels may be made of any material that is not porous, but it must be suitably dignified and durable. The Church does not usually allow glass or ceramic unless there are strong reasons of necessity, such as extreme poverty, dire emergency, or imminent danger in times of persecution.

The *paten* is a shallow dish, like a plate or shallow bowl, on which the bread is offered. Usually the upper surface is completely smooth and undecorated.

The *chalice* is the cup in which the wine is offered. It usually sits on a base that is broad enough to make the chalice comfortably stable when resting on the altar. The chalice can be elaborately decorated, as long as a smooth area is left around its lip.

The paten and chalice should be made of the same material, so that they obviously belong together. They must be consecrated, either by a bishop or by a priest designated by the bishop.

The *ciborium* is a vessel in which consecrated hosts are kept for later reception of Communion. The priest might use these hosts at a Mass when the crowd exceeds the number of hosts consecrated. The ciborium may look very much like a chalice, but it is usually broader and rounder, and it often has a lid with a cross on the top. The ciborium resides in the tabernacle.

A *monstrance* is a portable shrine for the Body of Christ, designed to make the Host visible for adoration while keeping it safe. It is used outside the Mass, for Eucharistic adoration and benediction.

A *pyx* is a small container for carrying the consecrated Host to the sick or to anyone who cannot come to church for Communion.

The *tabernacle* is a special box, often elaborately decorated, in which the Eucharist is kept. In modern churches the tabernacle is usually on its own altar. In larger churches it may have its own chapel, where the faithful can go to pray. The tabernacle should always be clearly visible and should occupy a prime place within the church.

53. What's special about altar candles?

There must be at least two altar candles lit during Mass. Some early theologians took this requirement so seriously as to hold that the Mass had to be begun again if the candles went out. Lighted candles represent celebration.

The candles are made from beeswax, the purity of which represents the pure flesh of Christ. The candlewick represents the soul of Christ, and the flame represents his divinity.

54. What are rubrics?

Rubrics are the instructions for the Mass. They're something like the stage directions in a play: Most of the Mass is made up of spoken words, but the rubrics tell us how those words are to be spoken and what the priest and other participants should be doing while they're speaking them.

The name *rubrics* comes from the Latin word for *red*, since—for as long as anyone can remember—these instructions have always been written in red ink, to distinguish them from the spoken text of the Mass. They're still usually printed in red in missals today, if the missals are printed in two colors.

The priest should follow the rubrics without improvising. The liturgy belongs to the Church, and it should be an act of humble service offered by both priests and laypeople. Improvisation, in any event, is often a symptom of an outmoded clericalism. As laypeople may not randomly offer spontaneous or idiosyncratic responses, priests too should do what the Church expects of them.

55. What's hidden in the compartment in or under many altars?

Altars often contain or are built over the relics of a saint. In Rome, for example, St. Peter's body lies under the altar of St. Peter's Basilica, and St. Paul's body lies under the altar of the Basilica of St. Paul Outside the Walls.

This is a tradition that goes back to the very early days of the Church. During the times of persecution, Masses were often celebrated at the tombs of the martyrs in the catacombs, on altars built over the relics of saints who had given up their lives for Christ.

In the visions recorded in the book of Revelation, John sees living saints under the altar in heaven: "When he opened the fifth seal, I saw under the altar the souls of those who had been slain for the word of God and for the witness they had borne" (Revelation 6:9).

56. Why does the Church honor the relics of the saints?

The relics of the saints are a connection with, and a constant reminder of, the great Christians who lived on earth before us and are now alive with Christ.

We don't worship these relics, but we do *venerate* them: that is, we show them respect, not because they are objects of worship but because they represent the holy saints who live in heaven, who in turn point us toward Christ. We know that, at the end of time, the bodies of these saints will also be glorified and taken into heaven.

The veneration of relics didn't begin with Christians. When Moses led Israel out of Egypt, he brought along the bones of Joseph, whose dying request had been to rest in the Promised Land:

> And Joseph said to his brothers, "I am about to die; but God will visit you, and bring you up out of this land to the land which he swore to Abraham, to Isaac, and to Jacob." Then Joseph took an oath of the sons of Israel, saying, "God will visit you, and you shall carry up my bones from here." So Joseph died, being a hundred and ten years old; and they embalmed him, and he was put in a coffin in Egypt. (Genesis 50:24–26)

> And Moses took the bones of Joseph with him; for Joseph had solemnly sworn the sons of Israel, saying, "God will visit you; then you must carry my bones with you from here." (Exodus 13:19)

In early Christian times the believers often risked their lives to retrieve the bodies of the martyrs, who had been tortured to death by Roman authorities. These were women and men whose deeds had shown their close connection with Christ, and now they had joined Christ in heaven. They were certain to pray ceaselessly for their friends still on earth; purified of every imperfection, their love would be boundless. Is it any wonder that the persecuted Christians treasured every connection with the holy martyrs?

When the Mass was celebrated on an altar built over the tomb of a martyr, it was a reminder of just how precious the Mass is to us. It's precious enough to die for, which is exactly what the martyrs did. And if they could die for the Mass, we surely can muster enough effort to get to church on Sunday.

In one of his sermons, St. Ambrose gave us a good summary of why we honor the relics of the saints. Ultimately it's because Christ himself has consecrated them.

> We honor the memory of the virtue that will never die.
>
> We honor the ashes that the confession of faith has consecrated. In them we honor the seeds of eternity.
>
> We honor the body that has shown us how to love the Lord, that has taught us not to fear death for his sake.
>
> And why shouldn't the faithful honor the body that even devils venerate—the body that they tormented in death, but that they glorify in the tomb?
>
> So we honor the body that Christ himself honored in the sword, and that will reign with him in heaven.[1]

Receiving Communion

57. Who may receive Holy Communion?
Whoever is in communion with the Roman Catholic Church and is not prohibited for some very good reason may receive Communion in any parish.

Someone who has been excommunicated (see question 68, What is excommunication?) or who is living in a state of serious sin cannot receive Communion. If the priest knows of any reason why someone should not take Communion, he has the duty to make sure that person does not receive. If you know of some serious unconfessed sin weighing down your soul, you should not take Communion until you have gone to confession and been absolved.

Children should be old enough to understand what they're doing before they receive Communion. Canon law presumes that they have that knowledge by the time they're seven years old, but the parish priest is responsible for determining whether a child is ready.

58. How should I prepare to go to Mass and receive Communion?

First of all, you should not have any sin weighing down your conscience. Go to confession and receive absolution. (The saints and popes recommend regular confession, at least once a month.)

You should observe the fast (see question 59, What is the Communion fast?). If you have any lingering attachments to small sins, take advantage of the Penitential Rite to turn your back on those. Remember that you're going to meet Jesus face to face, and you want to be cleaned up and looking your best, spiritually speaking.

Approach Holy Communion with the reverence that's appropriate for meeting God in person. Even your clothes should show respect. Fashions change; Jesus didn't leave a decree that men should wear their best togas, nor will the modern Church decree that neckties are necessary for salvation. But we can at least dress to show as much respect to Jesus in person, who will judge us on the Last Day, as we would show to someone we wanted to impress at a job interview.

59. What is the Communion fast?

Before we take Communion we're expected to fast—to abstain from food and drink—for a short time. The rule is to fast for an hour before reception of Communion. In most cases a good bit of that hour will be taken up by the Mass itself. (But it's better to fast for an hour before Mass begins, to avoid petty calculations.)

Water never breaks the fast, nor does any medicine you need to take. (Breath mints do, however.) The aged and the ill are not obliged to fast; neither are those who care for them.

The Communion fast is certainly not a serious hardship. It is just enough to remind us that something important is happening.

Fasting has always been an important part of Christian life. Jesus did it, and he assumed that his followers would:

> And when you fast, do not look dismal, like the hypocrites, for they disfigure their faces that their fasting may be seen by men. Truly, I say to you, they have received their reward. But when you fast, anoint your head and wash your face, that your fasting may not be seen by men but by your Father who is in secret; and your Father who sees in secret will reward you. (Matthew 6:16–18)

So the apostles fasted too. In fact, the New Testament associates the apostles' fasting with their ritual worship:

> While they were worshiping the Lord and fasting, the Holy Spirit said, "Set apart for me Barnabas and Saul for the work to which I have called them." Then after fasting and praying they laid their hands on them and sent them off. (Acts 13:2–3)

> And when they had appointed elders for them in every church, with prayer and fasting, they committed them to the Lord in whom they believed. (Acts 14:23)

We fast as a sign of repentance. Just as we fast to purify ourselves physically before medical procedures, so we fast before Communion to purify ourselves spiritually.

When we fast before Communion, our hunger becomes a kind of sacrament—not one of the seven sacraments of the Church but still, like them, a physical sign of a spiritual reality. The hunger we feel is a sign of our soul's hunger for Christ.

60. What if I forget and break the Communion fast?

Go to Mass anyway, but excuse yourself from Communion by simply staying behind in your seat. The sin isn't in breaking the fast but in taking Communion without fasting. (See question 72, What should I do if I go to Mass but cannot go, or choose not to go, to Communion?)

61. What happens if I receive Communion in a state of mortal sin?

That's a bad thing—catastrophically bad. In fact, it's a mortal sin in itself. You need to recognize the seriousness of what you've done and go to confession as soon as you can.

> For any one who eats and drinks without discerning the body eats and drinks judgment upon himself. That is why many of you are weak and ill, and some have died. But if we judged ourselves truly, we should not be judged. But when we are judged by the Lord, we are chastened so that we may not be condemned along with the world. (1 Corinthians 11:29–32)

St. Paul tells us just how serious it is to eat and drink judgment upon ourselves. But he also makes it clear that the Lord doesn't judge us because he's angry but to bring us back to him, "so that we may not be condemned along with the world." That's why we have confession.

62. How should I receive Communion?

In North America the common practice is to receive Communion standing, but you have the right to kneel if you wish. Kneeling used to be the common way for receiving Communion, and it shows special reverence for God. However, it may cause surprise in some priests, especially in places where the practice is uncommon. Whatever you decide, try to be sensitive to local custom, and always strive to be patient and kind to priests. Holy Communion is not the proper moment for a public act of protest.

You may also decide whether to receive the Host on the hand or on the tongue (see question 63, Why do some people receive Communion on the hand and others on the tongue?). If you receive on the hand, your hands should be clean. Hold up your right hand if you're right-handed, or your left if you're left-handed, and rest it on your other hand. Wait for the person distributing the Host to place it in your hand; don't reach out and take it.

The person distributing the Host will say, "The Body of Christ," and place the Host on your palm. You respond, "Amen," and bow slightly. Then carefully place the Host in your mouth.

If you wish to receive on the tongue, keep your hands down and folded, and allow the person distributing the Host to place it on your tongue.

If the Precious Blood is also being distributed to the congregation, the person holding the chalice will say, "The Blood of Christ." You respond, "Amen," and carefully sip from the chalice. Don't dip the Host into the chalice. If for some reason you can't or don't want to drink from the chalice, remember that Christ is completely present in the bread alone.

63. Why do some people receive Communion on the hand and others on the tongue?

The Body of Christ is the most precious thing in the world. It's very important that none of it be lost or disrespected in any way.

In times past it was the rule that people receive the Host on the tongue. There were several good reasons. First of all, the hands of priests are consecrated expressly for consecrating and touching the Holy Eucharist. Over time it seemed fitting that such contact should be reserved to consecrated hands.

But there were other reasons, too. Superstitious people sometimes hid the consecrated Host for use as a sort of magic talisman, which is a serious offense called sacrilege. This was less likely to happen if people in the congregation never had an opportunity to hold the Host.

And then there were practical reasons: In the days before indoor plumbing, workmen might come to church with very grubby hands, and placing the Body of Christ on the grime and grease would be very disrespectful. And the Host can be placed on the tongue in one simple movement, allowing fewer opportunities for accidents.

Although these reasons are still valid, the bishops of the United States, with the approval of the Holy See, have decided that it's safe and respectful to offer Communion in the hand to people who wish to receive it that way. Those who receive on the hand should take special care to ensure that no small particles of the Host remain on their hands or fall to the ground.

Many people prefer to receive on the tongue because they find it more fitting and reverent, or because they grew up with the custom, or because they'd rather not take the chance of accidentally mishandling the Sacrament. The general rule is that the person receiving, rather than the person distributing, should decide whether to receive on the tongue or in the hand.

64. Is it better to receive Communion under both species? Do I receive "more" if I do?

Because Christ is fully present in both the consecrated bread and the consecrated wine, you don't get any more grace if you receive both species than if you receive only one. In Western Catholic churches it's common to see only the consecrated Host offered to the congregation. But this is a rule of practice rather than an article of doctrine; Communion under both species or under only one is equally valid. You're not getting just half of Christ if you receive only the Host or, for that matter, only the Blood of Christ, as people with wheat allergies sometimes do (see question 51, What if my body can't take any wheat at all?).

65. What is *viaticum*?

Viaticum is Holy Communion given to someone in danger of death. *Viaticum* is a Latin word that means "the food you take on a journey"; it's nourishment for the journey from earth to the next life, a comfort in moments of physical or moral pain, and strength against temptation to despair.

66. Can the Church deny Communion to particular individuals? If so, when and how?

The Church denies Communion to anyone who has been excommunicated (see question 68, What is excommunication?). For example, those who have participated in an act of abortion—the mother, the person who paid for it, the medical personnel—incur automatic excommunication and should not present themselves for Communion. Excommunication is a serious penalty, so the Church is generally reluctant to impose it.

The priest has a duty to make sure Communion is not offered to anyone who is not allowed to receive it. If he knows of an obstacle to your receiving Communion, he will usually speak to you about it, explaining what the problem is and what you can do to overcome it. But priests are not infallible or omniscient. If you know of some impediment to your taking Communion that the priest doesn't know about, just stay in your pew and pray when Communion is offered. Then find the earliest opportunity to talk to the priest about the problem.

> Whoever, therefore, eats the bread or drinks the cup of the Lord in an unworthy manner will be guilty of profaning the body and blood of the Lord. Let a man examine himself, and so eat of the bread and drink of the cup. For any one who eats and drinks without discerning the body eats and drinks judgment upon himself. (1 Corinthians 11:27–29)

As St. Paul says, we should examine ourselves before we take Communion, because we're in a better position than anyone else on earth to know what's lurking in our souls.

67. Why are certain politicians allowed to take Communion even when they vote against Church teachings?

Sometimes we see public figures taking Communion when they seem to be violating the rules: for example, politicians who don't actively oppose abortion or who make public statements that disagree with Church teaching.

One of the principles of canon law is that penalties are a *last resort*. If a Catholic is straying from the true path, the Church has the duty to use every means in her power to bring the lost sheep back to the fold. In the case of a public figure, the bishops must also consider the public effect of their own actions. What message will they be sending about the Church by how they react to such provocations? Should they make a statement correcting the public figure's error but let him continue to take Communion, to show that the Church values mercy and forgiveness? Should they excommunicate him, to show how seriously the Church takes her teachings? It's not an easy decision.

To some bishops, erring on the side of mercy seems like the more Christian thing to do, as well as the course most likely to convey to the world what Christian love is like. Others, however, say that the greater concern should be for the sinner's scandalous effect on the public, who may grow confused or cynical about Catholic doctrine, devotion, and discipline. Sometimes, if a bishop has met privately with public figures and failed to persuade them to change, the bishop must refuse to admit them to Communion.

68. What is excommunication?

Excommunication is the separation of a person or group from the communion of the Church. Someone who is excommunicated cannot participate in the sacraments. This is the most serious penalty a Catholic can incur. Still, it is meant to be medicinal—to move the person who has incurred the penalty to seek reconciliation with God and the Church.

Some sins are so serious that they automatically bring on the penalty of excommunication—for example, willfully participating in an abortion. In these cases the very act brings on the penalty. In other cases the penalty is imposed only after someone has repeatedly refused to submit to Church authority.

Among the most common problems for North American and European Catholics are irregularities in marriage. If you've been married in a civil ceremony, in a Protestant church, or anywhere else where the ceremony wasn't celebrated as a *sacrament*—and you haven't received the Church's official dispensation—then you're not really married according to Church law. That means you're living in a state of serious sin and a very public one. The priest has a duty to refuse Communion to you until the marriage is celebrated properly.

Excommunication is a *penalty* but not a *punishment*. The Church isn't taking revenge on the sinner; instead the Church hopes that the excommunication will bring the sinner back to the path of righteousness. As soon as the sinner has made a penance that suits the sin, the Church welcomes him or her back.

If you are excommunicated, you can (and should) still go to Mass, but you should not present yourself for Communion.

Excommunication can be lifted only by the bishop or by priests who are authorized by the bishop. When there is a danger of death, however, any priest can absolve the subject from excommunication.

69. How often may I go to Communion?

We're allowed to take Communion twice in one day if the second time is at a Mass. The Church encourages frequent Communion but not to the point of overfamiliarity. Even though we strive daily for greater intimacy with Jesus, we don't ever want to take him for granted. We must never lose our sense that Holy Communion is a great event, an encounter with God—with the flesh and blood of Jesus Christ. That's why there's a limit.

The limit used to be once a day, but now the Church encourages us to take Communion if we happen to find ourselves at Mass a second time—for example, if we accompany unexpected guests to an evening Mass after we've already attended in the morning.

70. How often must I go to Communion?

You are required to take Communion at least once a year, during the Easter season—extending from the Easter Vigil to Pentecost Sunday. Going to Communion at Mass on another day can fulfill that annual obligation only if some serious emergency keeps you from going to Communion during the Easter season. Receiving Communion more often, of course, is better, but once a year is the absolute minimum.

71. What should I do after taking Communion?

After you return to your seat, there may be some quiet time before the liturgy continues. This is a time when you may feel particularly close to Christ, and you should take advantage of the opportunity to meditate on that closeness. Pray silently, and give thanks to God for his greatest miracle.

This is a very special moment in which God is sacramentally in your body and soul. With your own words tell him that you love him; thank him for coming once more to you and for his numerous blessings. It is good to have a small prayer book that can help you give thanks to God and ask him for various graces. Sometimes the prayers in the back of the pew missal can serve this purpose; sometimes too, the words of a favorite hymn.

When the quiet time is over, join the rest of the people in the prayers of the Concluding Rites.

72. What should I do if I attend Mass but cannot go, or choose not to go, to Communion?

Make sure those near you can get around you, and while they commune, you can kneel and pray.

Not going to Communion is always an option, and you shouldn't feel pressured to participate if you don't feel ready. There may be times when you feel yourself restrained by an unconfessed sin, a grudge, or some other troubling circumstance.

If you think it's better to stay where you are than to commune unworthily, by all means do so. Then find the earliest opportunity to confess, to make amends to your neighbor, or to do whatever you think is necessary to put you back in a worthy state.

73. Are Catholics allowed to take Communion in a non-Catholic church?

From a Catholic standpoint, there is no barrier to taking Communion in an Orthodox church; the Orthodox have validly ordained clergy, and they believe in the real presence and the miraculous change that takes place in the Mass. But we should respect the practices of that church; many Orthodox churches do not allow Roman Catholics to take Communion.

Many Protestant churches offer their communion to any baptized Christian, but a Catholic must decline the offer. The Eucharist is the sacrament that unites us all in the one, holy, Catholic, and apostolic Church. "The cup of blessing which we bless, is it not a participation in the blood of Christ? The bread which we break, is it not a participation in the body of Christ? Because there is one bread, we who are many are one body, for we all partake of the one bread" (1 Corinthians 10:16–17). Accepting communion at a Protestant church would be a sign of a unity that does not yet exist—however regrettable that may be.

Catholics can participate in many of the prayers and hymns of Protestant churches, but they must abstain (as politely as possible) from communion.

74. Are non-Catholics allowed to take Communion in a Catholic church?

Again, there is no barrier to Orthodox Christians' taking Communion in a Catholic church when they feel great need and do not have access to an Orthodox parish, and when their local Orthodox bishop does not prohibit them.

Protestants, on the other hand, may not take Communion in a Catholic church. As in the case of Catholics in Protestant churches, Communion would be a sign of a unity that does not yet exist, although we pray for it earnestly.

If you have Protestant visitors at your parish, be cheerful and welcoming. Explain to them before the Mass begins that only Catholics can take Communion; since many Protestant churches offer communion to any baptized Christian, the guests may not know that there is any restriction. Help them find their way through the missal. (If they come from a liturgical church like the Lutherans or the Anglicans, the service will be very familiar.) In these small ways you may help bring about that unity we pray for.

The Parts of the Mass

75. How is the Mass divided?

Traditionally there were two main parts of the Mass:

1. The *Liturgy of the Word,* or *Mass of the Catechumens,* in which we hear the Scripture readings and the homily and pray for the needs of the Church and the world. It was called *Mass of the Catechumens* because, in the early days of Christianity, the catechumens—people who were still learning the faith and had not yet been baptized—were allowed to be present only for this part of the Mass.
2. The *Liturgy of the Eucharist,* or *Mass of the Faithful,* in which we take Communion. It was called *Mass of the Faithful* because, in early centuries, the catechumens were dismissed before it began; only baptized Christians could be present for this part of the Mass.

The Liturgy of the Word corresponds to the synagogue liturgy that was current in Jesus' time; the Liturgy of the Eucharist is the "breaking of bread" that Jesus Christ instituted at the Last Supper.

In recent missals the two parts are each divided in two to

make two more sections: *Initial Rites* at the beginning of the Mass and *Concluding Rites* at the end of the Mass. That gives us four parts altogether:

1. Initial Rites
2. Liturgy of the Word
3. Liturgy of the Eucharist
4. Concluding Rites

In addition to these main sections, each part of the Mass has its own name, often taken from the first word of that section in Latin. Thus we have the *Gloria,* the *Credo,* the *Sanctus,* and so on.

So this is how a typical Mass goes in a Catholic church:

1. Initial Rites
The priest greets us using the words Christ gave his apostles in what we call the Great Commission, "in the name of the Father and of the Son and of the Holy Spirit" (Matthew 28:19). We say "Amen," and then comes the Penitential Rite (see question 77, What is the Penitential Rite?) and the *Gloria,* the hymn of the angels (see question 79, What is the Gloria?). Then comes the *Collect,* a prayer for the day that gathers together or *collects* the prayers of the whole congregation. (It's spelled the same as the verb *collect* but is pronounced with the accent on the first syllable: "COLlect.") The Initial Rites end with the Collect.

2. Liturgy of the Word
The Liturgy of the Word begins with the first Scripture reading, which on Sunday usually comes from the Old Testament (though in the Pentecost season it may come

from the Acts of the Apostles).

After the first reading comes a psalm, one of the ancient hymns of the people of Israel. This may be sung by a cantor or recited by a lector, with the congregation contributing a refrain.

On Sundays and holy days there is a second Scripture reading, usually from one of the letters in the New Testament.

Now it's time for the Gospel. Because the Gospel is the most important of the Scripture readings, we surround it with simple but meaningful ceremonies. We all stand. The priest, deacon, lector, or choir introduces the Gospel with the Alleluia, except during Lent (see question 81, What is the Alleluia?). The priest says a quiet prayer that he will be worthy to proclaim the Gospel; or if a deacon will be reading the Gospel, the priest prays for the deacon. The Sign of the Cross reminds us that this is the story of our redemption (see question 82, What is the gesture people make before the reading of the Gospel?).

Usually a homily or sermon comes after the reading of the Gospel. There must be a homily on Sundays and on holy days of obligation; a short homily is recommended on every other day, but it is not required. (See question 83, What is a sermon supposed to be?)

After the sermon on Sundays comes the Creed, by which we tell the world that we believe what we've just heard in the Gospel (see question 84, What is the Creed?). We conclude the Liturgy of the Word with a comprehensive prayer (see question 85, What is the Universal Prayer?) for specific needs of the Church, our parish, our nation, and the world.

3. Liturgy of the Eucharist

Now we come to the heart of the Mass—the Eucharist,

where we'll see the sacrifice of Christ on our own altar. Since this is the most important part of the Church's worship, it's surrounded with prayers and rituals that go back to the time of the earliest Christians.

The Liturgy of the Eucharist begins with the Offertory (see question 87, What is the Offertory?). Then comes the Eucharistic Prayer, of which there are several forms (see question 88, What is the Eucharistic Prayer?). In this prayer the bread and wine become the real Body and Blood of Christ. Then comes the Communion Rite (see question 95, What is the Communion Rite?).

4. Concluding Rites

After the distribution of Holy Communion, the Mass ends very quickly. The priest says a short prayer, pronounces a blessing, and then announces that the Mass is ended.

76. Why does the Mass begin with the Sign of the Cross?

Christ's death on the cross is the sacrifice that brought salvation to all of us. At the Mass that sacrifice is present on our altar. Our Sign of the Cross reminds us where we are and what we're doing.

77. What is the Penitential Rite?

The Penitential Rite is a public confession of our sins. It's important to approach the Mass with a pure heart. A few moments of silence give us a chance to think about what sins are weighing on us.

In the *Confiteor* we confess—in a general way—our sorrow for these sins. Dramatic gestures (we strike our breasts) and repetition ("my fault, my fault") remind us of how serious our sins are and how desperately we want to be rid of them. We ask our brothers and sisters and the saints in heaven to pray for us. Finally the priest enjoins us to pray that God will forgive all our sins and lead us to salvation.

The *Kyrie* is another prayer in which we ask God to have mercy on us: "Lord, have mercy. Christ, have mercy. Lord, have mercy." Some parishes still say this ancient formula in Greek, *"Kyrie eleison. Christe eleison. Kyrie eleison."* This was the one part of the liturgy where the Greek language stuck, even after the rest of the Mass was translated into Latin.

In this rite God forgives our venial sins. For the forgiveness of mortal sins, we must seek God's forgiveness through the sacrament of reconciliation.

78. Why do we pray to Mary and the saints?

When we pray to the saints, we don't pray to them the way we pray to God. Rather we ask them to help us with their prayers.

We often ask our friends and family to pray for us, because we know that God listens to every prayer. As Catholic Christians, we also know that some of our best friends are in heaven. In the Creed we say we believe in the *communion of saints,* meaning that we know that all God's faithful people are united in one community, whether they live on earth or have gone on to greater and fuller life in heaven (see question 84, What is the Creed?).

When we ask our friends in heaven for their prayers, we do so knowing that they have been perfected in love but that they once had lives like ours and understand exactly what we need.

79. What is the Gloria?

The Gloria is a hymn of praise that comes near the end of the Introductory Rites of the Mass, just before the prayer called the Collect. When we sing, "Glory to God in the highest," we join in the hymn the angels sang at Christ's birth:

> And suddenly there was with the angel a multitude of
> the heavenly host praising God and saying,
> > "Glory to God in the highest,
> > and on earth peace among men with whom he is
> > pleased!" (Luke 2:13–14)

80. How does the Church pick the Bible readings for each Mass?

The Church keeps a list of readings, called the *Lectionary*, for each day. The Lectionary we use now runs in a three-year cycle. If you go to Mass every day for three years, you will have heard almost the entire Bible read; then the cycle begins again.

Look closely at the readings on any given day, and you'll discover that they're all related. Often the readings from the New Testament comment on or explain the readings from the Old Testament. Sometimes they're all on the same theme. Or we may see a prophecy in the Old Testament, its fulfillment in the Gospel, and St. Paul's meditation on both in one of his letters. The Lectionary arranges readings that way to show us how the whole Bible is related: We see that God had a plan from the beginning, and we learn how that plan was carried out through history.

The Catholic Lectionary, by the way, has been adapted for use in many Protestant churches. So on any given Sunday, not only are all the Catholic parishes reading the same Scriptures, but many of the Protestants you know will hear the same in their churches. Perhaps that will give you something to talk about on Monday morning.

81. What is the Alleluia?

Alleluia is a Hebrew word meaning "Praise the Lord." It appears in the later psalms, which are long hymns of praise. These psalms were (and still are) an important part of the Jewish Passover meal.

For most of the year we chant the Alleluia to introduce the Gospel reading. During Lent we usually don't use the Alleluia, since Lent is a time of repentance, and "Alleluia" is a cry of joy. A suitable acclamation is sung instead, such as "Praise to you, Lord Jesus Christ!" In either case, a Scripture verse related to the Gospel is read by the priest or the lector or chanted by the choir, then the acclamation is repeated.

82. What is the gesture people make before the reading of the Gospel?

The priest makes the Sign of the Cross, first on the book of the Gospels and then on his forehead, his mouth, and his breast. The people should follow him in crossing forehead, mouth, and breast.

We make the Sign of the Cross on our foreheads to show that we publicly affirm our belief that Christ died on the cross to redeem us. We make the Sign of the Cross on our mouths to show that we confess Christ by our words. We make the Sign of the Cross over our hearts to show that we intend to take the Gospel teachings into our hearts and keep them there.

83. What is a sermon supposed to be?

A sermon or homily should reflect on the Scripture readings, explain them, and help us understand what they really mean for us. It should inspire us to live according to God's word as we've just heard it read from Scripture. This is why the sermon always comes after the Scripture readings in the liturgy: It continues the proclamation of the Word.

One of the oldest descriptions we have of the Christian liturgy comes from a book by St. Justin Martyr, who wrote in the middle 100s AD. Here's what he says about the Scripture readings and the sermon:

> And on the day called Sunday, everyone who lives in town or in the country comes together to one place, and the memoirs of the apostles or the writings of the prophets are read, as long as we have time for. Then, when the reading is finished, the leader gives us words of instruction, and urges us to imitate the good things we have heard.[1]

It would be hard to describe the purpose of a sermon more clearly than that.

Now, the priests who deliver our homilies are fallible human beings. They don't always hold our attention, and they don't always speak with perfect grammar or beautifully turned phrases. But they are our teachers, and we do need to listen to them when they speak to us.

Only a bishop, priest, or deacon is permitted to give the homily at Mass. Laypersons may teach and exhort at other moments and in other settings.

84. What is the Creed?

The Creed is a statement of Christian belief. The word itself comes from the Latin *credo*, "I believe."

There are two creeds we commonly use. The Nicene Creed is the longer one that forms part of our normal Mass; the Apostles' Creed is the shorter one that we use in certain rites.

The Apostles' Creed goes back to the very early days of Christianity. Although it carries the name of the apostles, it was not written by them. Rather it very succinctly presents the fundamental beliefs of Christian faith transmitted by the apostles to their successors.

By the early fourth century many heretical groups had spread false teachings about the nature of Christ. The Council of Nicea, which was called to clarify and define the true teaching of the Church, produced a creed that spelled out Catholic doctrine more specifically. That creed was refined, a few years later, by the Council of Constantinople. We know the final version as the Nicene Creed, although Church historians sometimes call it the Niceno-Constantinopolitan Creed, to distinguish it from the original version that came out of the Council of Nicea.

Both creeds are divided into three parts. The first part deals with God the Father, the second with God the Son, and the third with God the Holy Spirit. The second part in each is the longest, because our faith in Christ as God the Son is what defines us as Christians, and because most of the debates that the Nicene Creed was intended to settle were about the nature of the Son.

When we recite the Creed, we join ourselves with all the Catholic Christians all over the world who recite the same creed. We make a promise—to them, to ourselves, and to God—that we will hold ourselves to the teaching of the universal Church.

85. What is the Universal Prayer?

After the Creed we pray for the needs of everyone in the world. This prayer is also known as the Intercessory Prayer, the Prayer of the Faithful, or the Bidding Prayer. Following the order of charity, the first petition should always be for the Church and the Holy Father. Then there are petitions for political leaders, for our own congregation, for those who are sick or in trouble, and for all the people of the earth. We can and should add our own intentions in silence.

86. Why does the Church collect money at Mass?

The obvious answer is that the Church needs money—to take care of the poor, to keep up the buildings, to feed and house priests, and so on.

But the benefit is at least as much to ourselves as to others. Whenever we give from what we have, we join our sacrifice to the sacrifice of Christ. It's true that ours costs us very little compared to Christ's sacrifice, but it does us good to make it. The offering comes just before the celebration of the Eucharist so that, as we become one body with Christ, our gifts are joined with his gift of himself.

87. What is the Offertory?

The Offertory is a chant or prayer at the beginning of the Liturgy of the Eucharist. In it the priest offers the bread and wine to God, to be made into the Body and Blood of Christ. Prior to the Offertory, as the gifts of bread and wine are brought to the altar, Christians should offer themselves, their worries and joys, their work and leisure, to God to be taken up with Christ's perfect sacrifice.

The priest prepares himself with quiet prayers to offer the sacrifice and asks us to pray that he may be worthy to make the offering.

88. What is the Eucharistic Prayer?

The Eucharistic Prayer is actually a long series of prayers including the *Sanctus* and the institution narrative. There are several forms of the Eucharistic Prayer, so you won't hear the same words in every church you visit, and you may not hear the same words at every Mass in your own parish. All these forms, however, have the same basic elements.

The prayer begins with a greeting:

> *Priest:* The Lord be with you.
> *People:* And with your spirit.
> *Priest:* Lift up your hearts.
> *People:* We lift them up to the Lord.
> *Priest:* Let us give thanks to the Lord our God.
> *People:* It is right and just.

These very words have been used to begin the Eucharist in Christian liturgies since the earliest times. They're recorded in a liturgy written down in the early third century AD, which means they must have been in circulation for some time before that.

A *Preface* comes after this opening dialogue (see question 90, What is the Preface?), then the *Sanctus* (see question 91, What is the "Holy, Holy, Holy"?), the institution narrative (see question 92, What is the institution narrative?), and further prayers of praise and petition. The priest then holds up the large consecrated Host for all to see and proclaims a doxology, to which we respond, "Amen," often in song.

89. What is the Canon of the Mass?
In the Mass that was standard in the Western Church before 1970, the Eucharistic Prayer was called the Canon of the Mass. *Canon* is a Greek word meaning "rule," but the traditional name is so ancient that no one remembers exactly what "rule" the name refers to. The most plausible explanation is that the name was used to distinguish a standard Eucharistic Prayer that had replaced a number of local variants.

You may still see the older form of the Mass celebrated today (see question 44, What is the Tridentine Mass or Extraordinary Form?) in certain parishes, in which case the Eucharistic Prayer will be called the Canon.

The same prayer is still one of the optional forms of the Eucharistic Prayer, so even in the current Mass you will hear the First Eucharistic Prayer referred to as the Canon or Roman Canon.

90. What is the Preface?
The Preface is a prayer of praise that comes before the main Eucharistic Prayer and introduces the *Sanctus*, or

"Holy, Holy, Holy." It reminds us of all the reasons we have to praise God. In some forms of the Eucharistic Prayer, the Preface changes with the season, so that we always remember to praise and thank God for the saints or events in salvation history that we're celebrating on any particular day. In other forms the Preface is always the same, because the whole Eucharistic Prayer tells the story of salvation history.

91. What is the "Holy, Holy, Holy"?

The *Sanctus*, or "Holy, Holy, Holy," is another hymn of praise that we share with the angels in heaven. We hear it first in one of the prophet Isaiah's visions, where Isaiah sees the court of the Lord and the seraphim, who are the highest order of angels in the traditional Christian ranking:

> In the year that King Uzziah died I saw the Lord sitting upon a throne, high and lifted up; and his train filled the temple. Above him stood the seraphim; each had six wings: with two he covered his face, and with two he covered his feet, and with two he flew. And one called to another and said:
>
> "Holy, holy, holy is the LORD of hosts;
> the whole earth is full of his glory."
>
> And the foundations of the thresholds shook at the voice of him who called, and the house was filled with smoke. (Isaiah 6:1–4)

In the book of Revelation the "four living creatures"—who are clearly the same as the seraphim in Isaiah—sing a very similar hymn:

> And the four living creatures, each of them with six wings, are full of eyes all round and within, and day and night they never cease to sing,
> "Holy, holy, holy, is the Lord God Almighty,
> who was and is and is to come!" (Revelation 4:8)

The Hebrew name *seraphim* has to do with burning or *ardor*, which Christian writers like St. Thomas Aquinas have interpreted as referring to their burning love for God. So the "Holy, Holy, Holy" is really a hymn of love, attempting to express in words our burning love for the God who gave us our very existence.

Even before the year AD 100, we hear St. Clement urging the church in Corinth to join that angelic hymn, and some historians take his words as evidence that the Christians were already using the "Holy, Holy, Holy" in their liturgy:

> Let us submit ourselves to His will. Let us consider the whole multitude of His angels, how they stand ever ready to minister to His will. For the Scripture says, "a thousand thousands served him, and ten thousand times ten thousand stood before him" (Daniel 7:10), and they cried, "Holy, holy, holy, is the Lord of hosts; the whole earth is full of his glory" (Isaiah 6:3).
>
> Therefore let us also, conscientiously gathering together in harmony, cry to him earnestly, as if we had one mouth, so that we may be made to share in his great and glorious promises. For it says, "What no eye has seen, nor ear heard, nor the heart of man conceived, what God has prepared for those who love him" (1 Corinthians 2:9).[2]

To the hymn of the seraphim we add the praise the crowds shouted when Jesus Christ entered Jerusalem in triumph on Palm Sunday: "Most of the crowd spread their garments on the road, and others cut branches from the trees and spread them on the road. And the crowds that went before him and that followed him shouted, 'Hosanna to the Son of David! Blessed is he who comes in the name of the Lord! Hosanna in the highest!'" (Matthew 21:8–9).

Just as the crowds in Jerusalem heralded the arrival of the Messiah in their city, we herald the imminent arrival of our Savior on our altar.

92. What is the institution narrative?

The institution narrative, part of the Eucharistic Prayer, tells the story of Jesus' institution of the Eucharist at the Last Supper. It includes the words Jesus spoke when he gave the disciples his body and blood: "This is my body, which will be given up for you," and "This is the chalice of my blood, the blood of the new and eternal covenant, which will be poured out for you and for many for the forgiveness of sins." When the priest speaks these words, transubstantiation occurs: The bread and wine become the true Body and Blood of Christ.

The institution narrative we use in our liturgy comes from Scripture, but it isn't directly from any one book of the New Testament. Instead it puts together the accounts from the Gospels of Matthew, Mark, and Luke with the account St. Paul gives in 1 Corinthians 11. Since there are several variations of the Eucharistic Prayer (see question 88, What is the Eucharistic Prayer?), the institution narrative is not the same at every Mass. The story is always the same, of course, but it may be told in a more elaborate or more abbreviated way, depending on the setting.

This is the climax of the Mass, and the words of Christ in the institution narrative are so important that modern editions of the missal usually print them in capital letters to distinguish them from everything else in the Mass.

93. Why does the Church call upon the Holy Spirit at this point in the Mass?

When the angel Gabriel came to Mary to announce that she would bear a son, she asked him, "How can this be, since I have no husband?" The answer he gave her was

> The Holy Spirit will come upon you,
> and the power of the Most High will overshadow you;
> therefore the child to be born will be called holy,
> the Son of God. (Luke 1:34–35)

In that original miracle of the Incarnation, Christ, the Son of God, became flesh and blood through the action of the Holy Spirit. When that happened Christ was really present in the world as flesh and blood

In our Mass the priest asks for that miracle to be reenacted on the altar, once again through the action of the Holy Spirit. We're asking for nothing less than the Incarnation, Christ again becoming present on earth in flesh and blood. And through the Holy Spirit, which Christ promised would come to his followers after they could no longer see him (see John 14:26; Acts 1:8), we all become one body with Christ in the Church.

94. What is the "mystery of faith"?

Just after the institution narrative, the priest genuflects before the Sacrament and proclaims, "The mystery of faith." The congregation respond with some variation of Paul's words after his own version of the institution narrative: "For as often as you eat this bread and drink the chalice, you proclaim the Lord's death until he comes" (1 Corinthians 11:26). In Paul's words we have the most succinct expression anyone has ever come up with to describe the *mystery of faith*.

The mystery of faith, in the words of Pope Paul VI, is "the ineffable gift of the Eucharist that the Catholic Church received from Christ, her Spouse, as a pledge of His immense love."[3] It's a mystery because, without faith, we can't understand it at all, and even with faith we can not completely understand it until we reach our final home in heaven. The depth of love bound up in the Eucharist is simply beyond anything mortals can comprehend.

This is one place where we need to rely on revelation rather than reason. Reason can teach us quite a lot. It is possible to know through reason that there is a God and to understand many of the attributes of God. But although reason never *contradicts* the truth of Christian faith, reason alone can never reveal the *whole* truth. Because God wants us to know and love him completely, he reveals that truth through Scripture and the Church.

St. John Chrysostom, one of the most eloquent preachers the Church has ever known, told his flock to take Christ at his word even when they couldn't completely understand his sayings:

So let us believe God in everything, and contradict him in nothing, even when what he says seems to be contrary to our thoughts and senses. Let his word be of higher authority than both what we think and what we see. Let us do so in the mysteries also, not looking at the things set before us, but keeping in mind his sayings.

For his word cannot deceive, but our senses are easily beguiled. His word has never failed, but our senses go wrong in most things. Since, then, the word says, "This is my body," let us both be persuaded and believe, and look at it with the eyes of the mind.[4]

95. What is the Communion Rite?

The Communion Rite is the part of the Mass in which the Eucharist is distributed to the faithful.

All pray together the Our Father or Lord's Prayer. We offer each other the sign of peace, usually a handshake with the greeting "The peace of Christ be with you." This symbolically reconciles all our differences before we join in Holy Communion, as Christ instructed: "So if you are offering your gift at the altar, and there remember that your brother has something against you, leave your gift there before the altar and go; first be reconciled to your brother, and then come and offer your gift" (Matthew 5:23–24).

We then recite or sing the *Agnus Dei*, the prayer to the Lamb of God. The priest breaks the large Host and drops a small piece of it into the chalice with the Precious Blood. He holds the broken Host over the paten and says, "This is the Lamb of God who takes away the sins of the world. Happy are those who are called to his supper." We respond with the "Lord, I am not worthy" prayer (see question 97, What is the "Lord, I am not worthy" prayer?). Then the priest consumes a piece of the large Host and drinks from the chalice.

Now we receive Holy Communion. The priest, deacon, or lay Eucharistic minister announces to each person, "The Body of Christ," reminding us what the Host really is. If we're receiving both species, the minister announces, "The Blood of Christ," as we receive the chalice. Our response to both acclamations is "Amen!"

96. Why do we pray the Lord's Prayer at this part of the Mass?

In the Lord's Prayer we ask the Father to give us our daily bread. The bread we are about to receive is our spiritual sustenance, far more necessary to us than mere food. This is the real daily bread we should always be praying for, since "man does not live by bread alone" (Deuteronomy 8:3; see Matthew 4:4).

The Lord's Prayer is the prayer that Jesus taught his disciples when they asked him, "Lord, teach us to pray" (Luke 11:1). The Lord's Prayer begins by invoking God as Father, because that is who he is. Then it summarizes all the petitions that people make to God.

97. What is the "Lord, I am not worthy" prayer?

Just before we receive Communion, the priest holds the Host over the paten and says, "This is the Lamb of God who takes away the sins of the world. Happy are those who are called to his supper." We in turn pray, "Lord, I am not worthy that you should enter under my roof, but only say the word and my soul shall be healed." Like much of the liturgy, these words are taken from Scripture. St. Luke tells us of a centurion who wanted Jesus to heal his beloved servant:

> Now a centurion had a slave who was dear to him, who was sick and at the point of death. When he heard of Jesus, he sent to him elders of the Jews, asking him to come and heal his slave. And when they came to Jesus, they begged him earnestly, saying, "He is worthy to have you do this for him, for he loves our nation, and he built us our synagogue." And Jesus went with them. When he was not far from the house, the centurion sent friends to him, saying to him, "Lord, do not trouble yourself, for I am not worthy to have you come under my roof; therefore I did not presume to come to you. But say the word, and let my servant be healed. For I am a man set under authority, with soldiers under me: and I say to one, 'Go,' and he goes; and to another, 'Come,' and he comes; and to my slave, 'Do this,' and he does it." When Jesus heard this he marveled at him, and turned and said to the multitude that followed him, "I tell you, not even in Israel have I found such faith." And when those who had been sent returned to the house, they found the slave well. (Luke 7:2–10)

When the priest leads us in the "Lord, I am not worthy" prayer, we profess the same sort of faith that the centurion professed: that even though we are not worthy, Christ has the power and the authority to overcome all our unworthiness. It is a humble petition acknowledging our need for God.

98. What is Holy Communion?

Holy Communion is the actual Sacrament of the Eucharist, in which we take the consecrated bread or the consecrated bread and consecrated wine. It's called "Holy Communion" because it's the sacrament that unites us to Christ and makes us all part of the one body of Christ. It is the most precious gift that anyone can receive on earth. It is the Gift of Life, the Gift of God himself to his children.

99. Why does the Mass end so abruptly after Communion?

Holy Communion is at the end of the Mass because it is, in a sense, the end of history. The whole Mass has been leading up to this moment, because the whole of human history has been leading up to the point where God and humanity could once again be joined in communion. Holy Communion is an earthly foretaste, a beginning, of heaven.

Why does a movie end shortly after the villain is defeated, the problems are solved, and the hero and heroine get together? Why does a Shakespearean comedy end just after the last obstacle to a happy ending is overcome? It's because that's the end of the story. We can assume that time goes on after that, and the world continues to exist. But things are in their right places now; the drama has ended.

The Mass is the greatest drama in the world, because in a way more real than any play or movie, it makes the story of our salvation come alive in front of us. Like any good drama, it quite rightly ends shortly after its climax. What's left is to give thanks to God and to carry the grace we've received out into the world, where it will give us the strength to do God's will.

100. What should I do after Mass?

Take the power of the Mass out into the world.

What you've just been given is a miraculous gift—so miraculous that the greatest minds of all the ages have struggled to come up with words to describe it. You've become *one body* with Christ, and with all the other people of God. That includes the people in your parish, the billion or so Catholic Christians around the world, and all the saints who have ever lived.

"Because there is one bread," says St. Paul, "we who are many are one body, for we all partake of the one bread" (1 Corinthians 10:17).

One person can only do so much in the world. But with all these good people acting together, with Christ himself as our head, is there anything at all we can't accomplish?

Remember that you have a part in God's plan. The Mass unites us so that we can all work together. That doesn't mean each of us has to do everything; on the contrary, it means that each of us should be doing what God calls us to do.

Long ago St. Paul explained the idea, and no one has ever put it better than he did.

> Now there are varieties of gifts, but the same Spirit; and there are varieties of service, but the same Lord; and there are varieties of working, but it is the same God who inspires them all in every one. To each is given the manifestation of the Spirit for the common good. To one is given through the Spirit the utterance of wisdom, and to another the utterance of knowledge

according to the same Spirit, to another faith by the same Spirit, to another gifts of healing by the one Spirit, to another the working of miracles, to another prophecy, to another the ability to distinguish between spirits, to another various kinds of tongues, to another the interpretation of tongues. All these are inspired by one and the same Spirit, who apportions to each one individually as he wills.

For just as the body is one and has many members, and all the members of the body, though many, are one body, so it is with Christ. For by one Spirit we were all baptized into one body—Jews or Greeks, slaves or free—and all were made to drink of one Spirit.

For the body does not consist of one member but of many. If the foot should say, "Because I am not a hand, I do not belong to the body," that would not make it any less a part of the body. And if the ear should say, "Because I am not an eye, I do not belong to the body," that would not make it any less a part of the body. If the whole body were an eye, where would be the hearing? If the whole body were an ear, where would be the sense of smell? But as it is, God arranged the organs in the body, each one of them, as he chose. If all were a single organ, where would the body be? As it is, there are many parts, yet one body. The eye cannot say to the hand, "I have no need of you," nor again the head to the feet, "I have no need of you." On the contrary, the parts of the body which seem to be weaker are indispensable, and those parts of the body which we think less honorable we invest with the greater honor, and our unpresentable parts are treated with greater modesty, which our more presentable parts do not require. But God has so composed the body, giving the greater honor to the inferior part, that there may be no discord in the body, but that the members may have the same care for one another. If one member suffers, all suffer together; if one member is honored, all rejoice together.

Now you are the body of Christ and individually members of it. And God has appointed in the Church first apostles, second prophets, third teachers, then workers of miracles, then healers, helpers, administrators, speakers in various kinds of tongues. Are all apostles? Are all prophets? Are all teachers? Do all work miracles? Do all possess gifts of healing? Do all speak with tongues? Do all interpret? But earnestly desire the higher gifts. (1 Corinthians 12:4–31)

NOTES

Basics of the Mass, Questions 1–8

1. Thomas Aquinas, *Summa Theologica* 3, ques. 48, art. 3, *ad* 3, newadvent.org.

The Eucharist: The Real Presence of Christ, Questions 9–17

1. Ignatius of Antioch, Letter to the Smyrnaeans, chap. 7, www.newadvent.org.
2. Clement of Alexandria, *The Instructor*, bk. 2, chap. 2, www.newadvent.org.
3. Cyprian of Carthage, Epistle 62, no. 13, newadvent.org. Language adapted to modern English.

Scriptural and Historic Roots, Questions 18–25

1. Pliny the Younger, Letter 47 to Trajan, "On the Punishment of Christians." See A.N. Sherwin-White, *Fifty Letters of Pliny* (Oxford: Oxford University Press, 1969), pp. 176–177.
2. Justin Martyr, *First Apology*, nos. 65–66, newadvent.org. Language adapted to modern English.
3. Hippolytus of Rome, *The Apostolic Tradition*, part 4, author's adaptation based on the translations of Burton Scott Easton (1934) and Gregory Dix (1937).

Properly Equipped, Questions 48–56

1. Ambrose, Sermon 55, as quoted in Daniel Rock, *Hierurgia* (London: Hodges, 1892), p. 41.

The Parts of the Mass, Questions 75–100

1. Justin Martyr, *First Apology*, no. 67, new advent.org. Language adapted to modern English.
2. Clement of Rome, *To the Corinthians*, chap. 34, newadvent.org. Language adapted to modern English.
3. Pope Paul VI, *Mysterium Fidei*, Encyclical on the Holy Eucharist, no. 1, September 3, 1965, www.vatican.va.
4. John Chrysostom, Homily 82 on Matthew, no. 4, newadvent.org. Language adapted to modern English.